Your Career, Your Life

YOUR CAREER, YOUR LIFE

Career Management for the Information Professional

Edited by
Rosemary Raddon
with Angela Abell, Rossana Kendall
and Liz Roberts

ASHGATE

Published by
Ashgate Publishing Limited
Gower House
Croft Road
Aldershot
Hants GU11 3HR
England

Ashgate Publishing Company
Suite 420
101 Cherry Street
Burlington, VT 05401-4405
USA

Ashgate website: http://www.ashgate.com

British Library Cataloguing in Publication Data
Your career, your life : career management for the
   information professional
   1. Library science - Vocational guidance 2. Information
   science - Vocational guidance
   I. Rosemary Raddon
   020.2'3

Library of Congress Cataloging-in-Publication Data
Raddon, Rosemary.
   Your career, your life : career management for the information professional / Rosemary Raddon.
      p. cm.
   Includes bibliographical references and index.
   ISBN 0-7546-3634-8 (pbk.)
      1. Library science--Vocational guidance. 2. Information science--Vocational guidance. 3.
   Librarians--Employment. 4. Career development. I. Title.

   Z682.35.V62R33 2004
   020'.23--dc22
                                                                    2004041110

ISBN 0 7546 3634 8

Typeset by Owain Hammonds, Ceredigion.
Printed in Great Britain by TJ International, Ltd, Padstow, Cornwall

Contents

List of Contributors

ANGELA ABELL

Prior to joining TFPL in 1994, Angela held senior information management posts in the public, private and academic sectors. These include managing an information broking and consultancy company owned by the University of Hertfordshire, eight years as information officer for an engineering company and senior librarian at Huddersfield Polytechnic.

Since the mid-1980s, Angela has undertaken research and consultancy in areas associated with the management of information and knowledge and its impact on business performance. This includes the development of information and knowledge strategies, information auditing and knowledge mapping, and the development of skills and competencies needed in the knowledge economy. She is the joint author with Nigel Oxbrow, of *Competing with Knowledge*, published by the Library Association in 2001.

She is a visiting professor at the London Metropolitan University and on the advisory board of Sheffield University Department of Information Studies; a Fellow of the Chartered Institute of Library and Information Professionals (CILIP) and of the RSA; and a member of the Institute of Management Consultants and the Special Libraries Association (USA).

ROSSANA KENDALL

After teaching in universities and schools abroad and in the UK, Rossana Kendall trained as an information worker at the Polytechnic of North London. She then worked in academic libraries as an information/research officer, developing learning resources for managers. After taking up a post as a training officer in a public library service, Rossana completed a training to qualify as a psychodynamic counsellor. She currently has corporate responsibility for learning and development in a local authority in

London, and has completed a Masters degree in human resource development. Her particular interest is in applying psychodynamic concepts to the understanding of organizational life, and Rossana has published work on topics ranging from action learning to the meaning of buildings in library and information work.

ROSEMARY RADDON

After working in West Africa and the USA, Rosemary held a range of posts with the Inner London Education Authority. She was also Head of Library and Information Services in Hackney, and then moved into teaching in Higher Education, becoming Head of Library and Information Management at the Universities of Northumbria and North London.

She subsequently trained as a psychodynamic counsellor, and now works in the public and private sectors as a counsellor and careers adviser.

She has written extensively and travelled and worked as a consultant, teacher and trainer in the UK and overseas.

LIZ ROBERTS

Liz Roberts has substantial experience in local government management at a senior level and has undertaken national and regional roles in the Library and Information world. She has been involved with management issues for many years, has contributed to publications on management and organizational behaviour and has a particular interest in the dynamics of the relationship between individuals and the organizations they work within. Her qualifications include an Msc in Organizational Behaviour and a Diploma in Management Studies. She has recently decided to make a complete lifestyle and career change and is now a part-time English language tutor and a student, and is pursuing a range of new interests.

List of Figures

Introduction

The unexamined life is not worth living.

(Socrates, in Plato, *Apology*, 38A)

Work, with all that the word implies, tends to be a word that rarely provokes deep thought, although it is given a total of four columns in the Shorter Oxford English Dictionary, considerably more academic space than the thoughts, feelings and resultant actions that we usually attach to it. Yet these thoughts themselves run the whole gamut of human emotions, from anger and pain to pleasure and joy, or a mix of these and a multitude of other emotions. As our world of work is now changing at such a rapid pace, and within that world the information professions are changing equally rapidly, it seems an appropriate time to begin to examine the world of work, and the emotions, actions and decisions involved in this world. These issues are evoked by and acted out at work.

This book attempts to consider this world of work and careers, with particular reference to the library and information services (LIS) professions. It considers the meaning of work, the relationship between work and the worker, the range of choices available, how to make choices and, having made them, how to manage them and the resultant career. It also considers the needs of employers, the changing and developing skills within the LIS professions, the changing pattern of organizations, and ways in which professional workers can and should respond to these changes in order to develop their careers. Underpinning these issues are those of personal analysis and personal choice, so that work and worker support each other, rather than operating as separate entities. Career paths, career patterns, career choices and personal development have to be seen as a work and life relationship. Within this context, some key elements of psychodynamic thinking have been used to inform these closely linked areas.

The book is intended for young professionals, as well as those in mid-career who may be thinking of changing direction, or wondering if they should continue to develop their careers within the information world. It may also be of interest to students who are considering the careers available to them, and the implications to them personally of

1

the demands of employers and the skills they require. They may also wish to consider the dynamics of the range of organizations in which information professionals operate. Some of the implications for those who may opt for the individual/freelance option are considered, as these too are part of the overall career choice.

So the book aims to give support to the process of balancing work/career and self, through considering issues which are practical, as well as those which are more analytical, in order to give a complete and generally holistic perspective on the relationship between career and self.

The chapters progress logically, starting with considerations of work, linking these to individual perceptions and thoughts, then considering the relationship between worker and the workplace, making choices about this workplace, analysing the choices, processes and skills involved in career development, managing transitions, making decisions, and developing a career, or not. It tries to indicate a work pattern which is supportive and rewarding for the individual. These issues are set in the context of global and professional change. The book's main objectives are:

- To help individuals to make realistic and informed decisions about work and work contexts which are appropriate and relevant for *them*.
- To begin to identify the sets of skills, knowledge and personal qualities which are appropriate for the information professions and the information professional, and which can support careers and career development. It aims to give a developmental overview.
- To put issues into personal, work and organizational contexts, and into the larger social scene. It also aims to give a systemic and cultural overview.
- To provide an analysis of some of the unconscious issues that determine careers, their development and their context.

Overall the book tries to focus on a range of issues which inform the careers and career development of information professionals in a rapidly changing environment. It offers practical help and advice, sets this within the context of change, and in relation to the underlying psychodynamic issues which inform and contribute to change.

1 Work: overview and philosophy

Rosemary Raddon

The Second Coming! Hardly are those words out
When a vast image out of Spiritus Mundi
Troubles my sight: somewhere in sands of the desert
A shape with lion body and the head of a man,
A gaze blank and pitiless as the sun
Is moving its slow thighs, while all about it
Reel shadows of the indignant desert birds.
The darkness drops again; but now I know
That twenty centuries of stony sleep
Were vexed to nightmare by a rocking cradle,
And what rough beast, its hour come round at last,
Slouches towards Bethlehem to be born?

(W.B. Yeats (1919), 'The Second Coming', in *Collected Poems*, London, Macmillan, 1950, pp. 210-11). (By permission of A.P. Watt on behalf of Michael B. Yeats)

CONTEXT

Careers and lives are usually rooted in some way in the world of work, and this changing phenomenon of work forms the outer layer of a complex system. Work is one of the main external drivers in an intricate system containing a range of smaller systems, sub-systems, relationships, possibilities and personal responses to all of these. All interact with each other and are interrelated. At the centre is the individual psyche, with its own specific history, experiences and responses.

The changes in the drivers, form, content and structure of work have been evolving since the first exchange of goods and labour existed, but within the last century the pace of this evolution has accelerated, and information and the information professions have been among some of the most rapidly changing areas. These changes have been taking place in a context of social, economic and technological flux, linked to realignment of political ideologies. Globally these changes have included a rapid increase in competition, cross-border networks, the reduction of fixed places and systems in relation to finance, to systems which are now connected through technology, shifts in political interventions and the decay of some larger states and the rise of others. All these in turn link to alterations in the places where goods are produced, with some areas of the world decreasing in power, and others becoming increasingly important as sources of cheap labour and expertise, thus altering global relationships. Migrations and work patterns have also changed. Work and technological changes have then occurred as a result of these shifts, bringing alterations in linked social structures. Societal changes have also been part of these shifts, and organizations in turn have changed to reflect the changing global pattern.

Organizations have responded through the increasing use of technologies, changing formal structures, decentralization, improved flexibility, structural alterations in the workforce, and different responses to issues of race and gender. There is more stress on partnerships and the importance of stakeholders, and more flexibility and lateral thinking. Portfolio working is no longer innovative and new, and careers are not hierarchical and rigid. At the same time the gap between some countries and trading communities and others is widening. Political and religious movements are contributing to this gap, and tensions arise between traditional capitalist issues and values, and those of increasingly articulate alternative movements. All are supported and fuelled by global information systems and technological infrastructures. These support or may drive service or manufacturing economies or systems. These systems have and are in turn affecting economic, social and political movements. A survey of the national press of the United Kingdom of the last year will yield endless examples of these symbiotic processes. All contribute to the ever-changing and increasingly rapidly changing world of work.

The information professional, like other technological professionals, is an integral part of these changes, responds to them in a variety of personal and professional ways, and cannot be isolated from them. Perception of work and career satisfaction takes place within this broader picture of the so-called information society and of information technologies. Change and changing values, differing impacts, changing and diverse patterns of work and organizational shifts have to be managed and utilized, in relation to individual needs and aspirations. These individual needs and aspirations have to be seen within the wider context or system, but also within the context of a particular situation, organization or country. There has to be an analysis of the individual situation and of the particular structural framework. Such an analysis prevents individual needs and expectations being acted out or phantasized about within a seductive and over-simplified organizational or global framework. Managing self and the individual career requires such an overview in addition to the ability to focus on the specific.

THE WORLD OF WORK

Work is an integral part of most of our lives, experienced in many ways. The range of these experiences is rich and varied, and the words and phrases used to describe work and the emotions attached to it indicate that range. Students and workers use descriptors such as responsibility, realization, fulfilment, discipline, ideology, commitment, hurt, anger, pleasure, unemployment, fear, rejection, slavery, love, transformation, harassment, money, creation, family, alienation, defence, economics, bureaucracy, development, offensives, confidence, control, and many others. These free association descriptors indicate some of the experiences of work, expressed in external reality and in the ways in which work brings deep feelings to the surface. It can be seen that work can be experienced as day-to-day reality in a variety of ways, which may range from pleasure and rich rewards to boredom, pain, rejection and possibly unemployment. It can also be experienced as a phantasy (the perfect job/manager/organization existing somewhere at the end of the rainbow) of personal or other aspiration, as the fulfilling of ambition (real or imagined), or as compulsion, arising from internal unconscious drives or undertaken to satisfy the ambitions of another. It may be experienced as an alternative fulfilment for other unfulfilled needs, as an antidote to failure in other areas of life, as a result of social or peer pressure or relationship issues. It may also be experienced as the source of sophisticated material pleasure, kudos or esteem, or as the opposite – the ultimate yet unobtainable goal and the source of endless rejections.

So work can be experienced at many levels. Some of these levels are clear and often universal. Most of us have to work to survive economically – the reality of having to deal with the economics of living are observable and part of a complex social system. Decisions on work, families, location, levels of spending, loyalties, choices within or outside the system, are made and informed to a large extent by work. In addition to these concrete observable choices, other choices are made at a more unconscious level. Work gives many of us a role, an identity, a framework and the ability to operate within an acknowledged social system. Either overtly or covertly, many people perceive work as some kind of contribution to their society or environment. It makes some contribution to the eternal question 'what is it all about?' and provides a contextual process which provides a framework for an activity which occupies major elements of time. The degree to which these choices, and therefore needs, are met by the world of work depends on the degree of sophistication of the understanding of our own internal make up, and how this affects our working lives. Work is to some extent also determined by gender, and the social and political constructs which are built around this. Career choice is also affected by gender to some extent, and may be considered to be pertinent in the area of information management, as part of a tradition of the 'caring professional' with all the gender implications of that concept. Role models, behaviour and expectations are also influenced heavily by these constructs around issues of gender.

Work and our choices within the world of work also drive other processes. The desire for promotion helps contribute to continuing professional development, to acquiring additional qualifications, to enhancing existing skills or to acquiring new ones, to being professionally active, to supporting other members of the professions, to being mobile, to enabling workers to have a wide range of experiences in different organizations and locations, and to enhancing their economic leverage. Conversely, choices are made which reflect different internal needs and drives. Decisions may be made which avoid promotion, responsibilities, large organizations, decision making or professional development, and which concentrate very much on personal and/or family or community pleasures and interests.

For some, work and the world of work is a clear indication of social standing and meaning (indicated by social status or salary, and therefore 'worth') or aspiration, linked to a strong need for recognition of the self. For some it represents status or power. It may also be an avenue to obtaining approval if this is important, which has not been given by significant others, such as parents or partner. For others, work symbolizes control, as indicated earlier. It can also be an identity, where work and the person become one and the same, and are not differentiated. It can also be used to demonstrate competitive elements of the persona which cannot be expressed elsewhere in the family or social context, but which are safely expressed at work. It may be a way of establishing and expressing self-esteem and satisfaction, if this is not possible elsewhere. Work may also be a symbolic safety net, where a job which can be well done counterbalances real or imagined failures in other parts of a person's life. Fear of failing in relation to family, parents or children can be compensated for in this way. For the majority it is, however, a real economic driver, representing economic and personal security, as well as familial economic security. Unions are also playing an increasingly important role in career development, recognizing that this supports economic growth for their members, as well as social cohesion.

WORK AND SELF

Such experiences are different for all of us, but it is clear that there is a complex range of ways in which work is used to express thoughts and feelings. Some are clearly observable, while others are more complex or more effectively disguised. The differences in observable behaviours are a result of our own experiences and backgrounds, as well as our own intellectual, emotional and psychological frameworks. An understanding of some of these experiences and the feelings which fuel our behaviour and ambitions, enable us to begin to accept some of our strengths and weaknesses and to begin to see work as part of our own persona.

Professional cultures and organizations are outward expressions of the individual. They reflect human experiences in a range of contexts. The results of these engagements may be pleasure or pain, or conflict or resolution. The engagements may result in satisfactory careers or work experiences, or merely an unsatisfactory set of economic experiences. An understanding of some psychoanalytic theories can help to illuminate conflicts, difficulties and pleasures, and recognize some of the ways in which work and organizations affect workers and their careers. It can also help to illuminate the relationships between the individuals and career development.

Through an understanding of some of these theories, the external reality of work experiences can be seen to illustrate some of the many ways in which work expresses internal symbolic experiences. These internal experiences underpin the actual experiences, decisions, choices and developments at work. So the external becomes a manifestation of the internal, experienced at unconscious levels.

One clear example is the worker who seeks perfection, and who perceives control of events, people, organization or other elements at work as a way of achieving this perfection. This may relate to a range of experiences, probably including not having been valued sufficiently as a child or adolescent. Work then becomes a way of dealing with this strong need for recognition and approval.

So it can be seen that the world of work is both real, in its relationship to external experiences and organization, observed and observable, and unreal, in that it reflects individual and unseen internal needs and experiences. The process of linking these two elements and understanding their relationship is key to understanding the individual career. For the individual, the choice of work and career, the drivers which help to determine choices, the progression of career, or the lack of career, change of career, or maintaining several careers, or the abandonment of career, reflect both these real external worlds, and the individual internal worlds.

For the information professions, as for other professions, work now takes place within a rapidly changing environment. Everyone is aware of these changes in the post-modern world, touched on above. These also include consumerism and customization, technology, knowledge management, virtual organizations and experiences, public/private partnerships, competition, changing cultures, a recognition of the importance of research, stakeholder involvement, competitive organizations, and the resultant creativity as well as the tensions and paradoxes that these produce. Within this context, the further exploration of the relationship between the identified external realities and internal issues provides the basis for this first chapter. The book then continues to focus on a range of issues which inform and affect the careers and career development of information professionals within this rapidly changing environment.

As suggested in Figure 1.1, linked to these elements of change are the parallel changes required in the workforce and the individual. Changing work requires changing skills and competencies, as well as personal attributes. Qualities such as leadership, creativity, versatility, flexibility, team working and political awareness have been identified by employers, employers' federations and anyone involved in managing

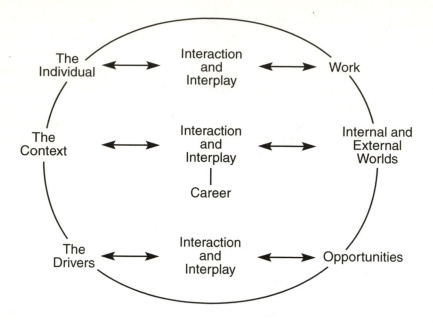

Figure 1.1 The information professional in the working world

workers in a context of change. Key skills and competencies such as management, transferability, financial ability, communication and interpersonal and political skills, to name but a few, have also been identified by employers in feedback and reports. These identified changes are followed by the debates on where and when and how they can be clearly identified, developed, transferred, imbued, offered as training, developed as part of career development, learned through experience or through academic routes. The growth in MBA degrees is an illustration of the need to support such changes within a formal framework. The debates also cross more traditional professional boundaries by identifying personal qualities, specific cognitive transferable skills (technological and organizational), linked by the phantasy of what is needed in the 'ideal' worker and workforce.

Individuals are increasingly having to analyse themselves in relation to the changing environment. This involves identifying gaps and weaknesses, developing these and then moving into advanced or new areas of expertise. Talent management is a key element for the modern information worker. This process is encouraged by forward-thinking employers as creative employees contribute to developments. The drivers shaping and determining these changes and debates are universal, including those identified earlier, and others such as the need for flatter and more flexible organizations, profits, market forces, political policies, and the management of and access to information. They all affect career development and organizational development as well as personal change.

They also inform debates on careers, as well as providing creativity or tension. Resolving tension can in turn lead to further creativity.

Accepted psychodynamic theories form the basis for the exploration of the relationships between the external observable and real world of work, and the more difficult area of the unconscious world. The majority of psychodynamic theories stem largely from the work of Freud, as well as from earlier work which he incorporated into his research. Many developments in thinking have taken place since then, and some concepts negated, but some core concepts remain unchanged. The basic premise is that individuals operate in two differing but interacting worlds. Both can be identified, and they interact with each other in different ways for different individuals. The external world is largely the conscious world in which work plays such a large part. The inner world, largely unconscious, strongly influences the actions and choices in the external and work-based world of the individual.

As already indicated, these worlds are dynamically linked, and usually are in some kind of balance or equilibrium. Some experiences and choices at work can alter or upset this balance, and some understanding of the relationship between the two worlds makes it easier to cope with conscious decisions made at work or home. Work tends to occupy much of an individual's time; and the relationships within work, perceptions of the self, perceptions of the organization, of the other workers, expression of emotions, the need to achieve, or not, are all expressions of the dynamic between these worlds.

In the world of work, careers and career development, there are many clear manifestations of these relationships between what is seen and done, and the underlying personal drives that lead to these behaviours and work and career patterns. If some of these familiar patterns can be analysed and recognized, they can provide a basis for further consideration of such relationships. This then supports career development and growth. It is of course important to distinguish between superficial analyses and more detailed personal explorations, but some patterns do reoccur, and can support further personal and organizational exploration.

Some of the descriptors used above can be grouped into positive experiences (development, fulfilment, commitment, love, transformation) or negative experiences and feelings about work (unemployment, fear, rejection, slavery), while others describe the sense of being caught up in a network which can submerge the individual. These feelings are part of an even more complex set of emotions, but within all of these are some clear threads which emerge in patterns of behaviour at work, and which are the result of internal emotions.

WORK – POSITIVE PROCESSES AND EXPERIENCES

For many people work can be a very positive and enriching experience. For example, it frequently provides a learning framework, where development can take place. This may

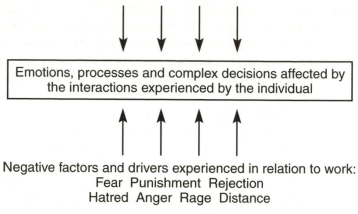

Positive factors and drivers experienced in relation to work:
Development Care Support Love
Achievement Growth Praise

Emotions, processes and complex decisions affected by
the interactions experienced by the individual

Negative factors and drivers experienced in relation to work:
Fear Punishment Rejection
Hatred Anger Rage Distance

Figure 1.2   Positive and negative influences on the individual

not always be clear, consistent or necessarily overt, but social interaction can be a learning process and help develop communication – a key transferable skill. Work can provide a sense of security and containment, and this is particularly important for workers who may have had difficult or interrupted educational patterns. The experience of managing the process of work within any organization is an important learning curve, enabling workers to respond to change. Skills which can be acquired through a learning framework represented by the organization can also be key transferable skills enabling the worker to choose the next place or context of employment. (The identification and development of transferable skills which are considered to be 'core' are explored in depth in Chapter 5 by Angela Abell.) Those personal and identifiable qualities which are enhanced through a sensitive and reactive organization, which may include professional development, coaching and mentoring, can be a positive and enriching experience. Continuing professional development can be sustained throughout a learning organization, but programmes can also be contrived for individual workers, contributing enormously to their personal growth. These are all supportive mechanisms, contributing to a positive and integrated experience. (Rossana Kendall considers organizational aspects of work in Chapters 6 and 7, and explores these dynamics further.)

Work and the workplace is also a very important social organization – it allows social interaction, relationships, friendships, frameworks, communication and a strong sense of belonging. These behaviours are crucial to most people, and if not available at work, will be constructed elsewhere as they are part of a strong social drive. These elements are also important in the current climate of homeworking, where these patterns are missing. Alternative ones can be sometimes contrived to take their place, but the social importance of work cannot be underestimated.

Work can also be a space where creativity and inventiveness can flourish. A supportive manager or organization can provide a strong creative framework. For the worker who has an awareness of his or her psychic framework, this can be a really important part of his or her development. To be allowed to develop, experiment, monitor, create and generally initiate in the workplace can be extremely rewarding. Such creativity can stem from personal innate creativity, or from the tension which may be created by the relationship between the inner and outer worlds. Alternatively the inability to manage such tension can produce dissatisfaction at not being able to manage conflicting needs. From this dissatisfaction can spring enormous creativity, the result of imaginative solutions to this state of dissatisfaction. New ideas, designs, systems and services may all be used in the drive to create something real for the external world. This reality will then satisfy internal needs also. So for creative people work can become a vehicle which allows them to express ideas in concrete form.

WORK – NEGATIVE PROCESSES AND EXPERIENCES

The flexible and imaginative work organization and management structure can support such creativity and utilize and develop it. But it can be ignored and subdued in less sensitive contexts, and negative elements and experiences can then detract from positive career development.

Such other experiences and emotions can lead to different patterns. For example, the need to gain approval through the workplace and to achieve at work can often be seen as a result of parental lack of approval, or of constant criticism. This may be submerged, and not necessarily acknowledged, but forms a strong driving force for some who want to achieve status and economic benefits. Such striving for approval may be linked to parental approval, but can also be a result of clear sibling rivalry, and the need to prove that he or she is good enough or better than the sibling that supplanted them in the affections of the parents. The behaviour of young children when presented with another sibling is clear evidence that such events produce strong emotions which can lead to radical change of behaviour. If not contained, then these feelings will continue to emerge and cause discomfort throughout adult life. Such feelings are rooted in real experiences, and become reinforced at every stage of development. Competition at school or university may follow and may be very evident later at work, but achievement may not necessarily be rewarding. Such competition can displace other aspects of work, and detract from any satisfaction, as the person will never achieve to the standard which he or she imagines is necessary. The competition may be denied and disguised by social competences, material sufficiency and family activities. Overall, the striving to be accepted at work and for general and professional approval often compensates for the perceived or actual earlier lack of recognition.

Strong ambition which is not inherently or clearly rewarding can also link to earlier experiences of a similar nature. This can be seen to be part of the need to please or subsume the self in order to gain approval, and so through constant striving it may lead to the construction of a persona and then a career which is unreal or 'false'. When such a career comes to an end, this can be devastating to the worker, because the façade is all that is left. The striving is another result of the need to be recognized and contained. This may or may not be realized by the person concerned: if identified and used, such striving can be creative and positive, but it can also be negative if it is unrecognized.

The outward manifestations of these internal emotions and experiences are thus a way of coping with emotional needs or distress, and are the individual's own personal defences used to cope with, manage and/or disguise these needs. The creativity and dedication may however not provide any or sufficient pleasure because of the need to be 'perfect'. This state is almost impossible to achieve, but the need to try and achieve continues to add to the sense of being driven. In their most sophisticated form, the origins of these drives and patterns of behaviour may be difficult to identify, as they may also produce equally sophisticated and creative patterns of behaviour and work, even though these are ultimately unsatisfying.

The world of work is frequently chosen as a place where this unconscious need for recognition and approval can be met. Within the information professions the sector choice, or even the specific organization, can be chosen to reflect need. A worker can choose to be part of a highly competitive organization, where achievement is clearly recognized, or strive for more and more senior posts, so that the obtaining of these is a clear recognition of ability, but made and acknowledged in the public arena. The need to achieve can also affect other relationships, including marital and family relationships, and generating a desire for these to be perfect. Conversely, such emotions can be very threatening to the self – if there is no work and no recognition and no outward manifestation of perfection, then what is there? A recognition of some of these issues can be very illuminating and remove some of the fear which controls the driving.

Another relatively familiar pattern of behaviour is that of control, evident in many information professionals. There is a need to distinguish between the need for control as part of data collection, processing, management and utilization, and control as a need for personal ascendancy, practised in an overall atmosphere of authority. The information professional can then become almost obsessive about rules and regulations, use of materials or use of data as a way of manifesting his or her own need. This may relate to feelings of insecurity, anger, anxiety, envy and many others. To be able to cope with this gamut of difficult feelings, they are projected into work and the workplace, and work and the control of systems and information are used as a way of controlling individual emotions. This is rarely acknowledged, but can be frequently observed. A career using systems as defences as a support for those with poorly integrated internal worlds is very evident in the information world. The need for control is exhibited and managed in the workplace, and demonstrates the way in which many workers are unable to cope with and acknowledge elements of their internal or unconscious worlds. These elements also relate to the incapacity of some people to tolerate anxiety and uncertainty. This frequently derives from inadequate support systems which were experienced during the formative years. Many people with the need for control can also be seen to be working overtime, denying their need for holidays, and always wanting to be seen as key to the organization. This gives them a feeling of self-worth, security and, above all, of really being in control. So work and life become totally linked: once work ceases, life becomes threatening at many levels as the defences cannot be utilized. The creative elements of work are thus denied, and work becomes difficult and negative, with anger being projected into all aspects of work and the workplace, as it cannot provide the internal security that is needed. The lack of creativity also contributes to feelings of negativity.

OTHER ISSUES

An important area of work is that related to gender. In theory the glass ceiling has cracked, but this is a simplistic view of a more complex situation (Davidson and Cooper, 1992). Many organizations are in theory equal in opportunities offered, but this assumption does not take into account all of the complex issues relating to gender, class, age, work and the relationship of these to careers.

Achievement in the information professions by women is still unbalanced in relation to the proportion of women in the workplace relative to men. However, some women have made clear decisions that work satisfaction is more important than promotion, and so do not seek to achieve positions of seniority. They may also have decided that family and community are, for example, more personally rewarding and satisfactory than workplace seniority (Poland et al., 1995). Some workers, as explored by Liz Roberts in Chapter 8, make clear decisions about careers in relation to personal values. The case studies also illustrate some clear personal choices.

Other issues relate to work as a vehicle for processing feelings, often unconsciously. For example, some workers express their feelings very clearly through work. 'Good' management is idealized, and can do no wrong. Management is experienced as the ideal and caring universal mother. Other managers are demonized and are unable to do anything that is perceived as good. Such projections may indicate an emotional immaturity, projected into and expressed through others. Those denigrated or to whom feelings are vented in a very aggressive way, may also represent the need for the worker to actually have some of those very qualities which are being ridiculed. It would be too difficult to acknowledge need or jealousy, and so anger is used as a defence or shield.

Sometimes the use of language supports feelings in a very graphic way. The choice of words clearly expresses personal emotions, triggered by experiences at work. It is often said of managers, or subordinates, 'he, or she, is a pain in the neck'. That pain in the neck and shoulders is often very real, and the physical pain is generated by emotional stress. Or 'he makes my toes curl up' is another familiar cry. Or, when in real distress, 'I'm on the edge', or 'I was rigid with fear' – a primitive physiological reflex response to danger, real or imagined.

Women may seek to achieve because compulsive achievement provides a strong internal sense of self and security. This need may stem from a lack of parental support, or the need to be more effective at work than a male sibling. Parental expectations may act as strong drivers, leading to senior office, but the anxiety resulting from this may cause enormous internal turmoil. The worker will ask questions of herself about her achievements – is she really good enough at work, and really good enough to get that much-needed approval? If there are major elements of self-doubt in senior women, it can be tempting to sabotage work, and destroy a job before it emotionally destroys them, thus leaving *them* in control, not the work. Over-compensation may result in personal difficulties, such as the ability to enjoy holidays, take time off, enjoy relationships, or simply relax and be creative. The internal or unconscious world of the individual is, in these cases, strongly influencing behaviour at work, and preventing development at a personal level. These defences then contribute at a very deep level to the lack of a sense of purpose. The vacuum can thus be filled by compulsive working and driving ambition, with organizations providing the setting for this.

Women from minority ethnic groups or those who have recently arrived in Western Europe as a result of global migrations also have these issues to contend with. In addition, many feel the need to achieve in order to vindicate some of the emotions of their families, who are trying to settle in new and different countries from those of their birth. Non-achievement is both a personal rejection, and also a cultural rejection. Achievement also carries a double burden with it – to fail is to be rejected by both organization and the community. Group projections and phantasies may be carried by individuals, and these can be difficult to manage and control so that the self is not overwhelmed.

It is important to recognize that work and career will not provide all the answers to life, and moving away from a strong position of defence, using work as a mechanism, to one of acceptance of self is difficult and long. For some workers, support may be needed for this process, either from family and friends, therapist, or through mechanisms at work. This recognition of the symbolism of work is central to the concept of career development, which aims to support a career, while at the same time placing it in the context of both the internal and external realities of the information worker's persona.

The experienced career counsellor can help interpret some of these dynamics, and so enable workers to begin to analyse and process individual patterns of living. These can then begin to make a kind of narrative for the individual which has a thread and a meaning to it, and thus inform future decisions and thoughts. Narrative, in a contained setting, can be a very useful and powerful form of self-exploration, which can support career management and development. 'Narrative turns experience into a story which is temporal, is coherent and has meaning' (Holmes, 1993, p. 150). Self-knowledge and self-identity are used as key elements in this process. Careers and work then become more meaningful and more easily set in familial and cultural contexts. Bringing together disparate and split elements of the self helps in the decision-making process and is personally supportive.

Career development thus links logically to career and work choice. These issues in turn are affected by political debate and events, and by social changes. The impact of globalization and increasing technology has philosophical implications for career choice and personal beliefs. Such choices are made in the contexts outlined above, of changing economic and work patterns, and also of a much more fluid and cross-cultural and geographical approach to careers and work, challenging many previously held career and work assumptions. Skills sets and assumptions have to change more rapidly within this changing work environment.

CAREER CHOICE AND CAREER GUIDANCE

Career choice is initially determined by a complex range of factors, including parental influences, social norms and values, role models, and school or college education and guidance. Class, gender, age and race will play a key role, as will other social variables. The curriculum itself will also play a part in career choice. Key people in the individual's own world, at home and at school or work will also play major roles, either overtly or covertly. Major emotional experiences will also contribute to choice. The effects of changes in national and international drivers will affect choices, such as major drives to recruit into particular professions or skills, and some of these campaigns will have an impact on those involved in information giving.

Career guidance can also play a major role, and the careers service is a key player in the world of work (Institute of Career Guidance, 2001). The interaction between career counsellor and worker will operate at the external information-giving level, involving two people in a close relationship. Any such relationship will then bring into play the hidden and unconscious worlds of those involved. For example, any professional will have his or her own traumas to deal with at any one time, but it is important to be aware that any such personal issues belonging to the counsellor may distort or manipulate information and advice giving, even if at a very superficial level. These personal issues must be clearly excluded from the process as far as possible. The worker may equally well have a particular set of desires and influences at a particular time – envy, competition, reparation, and his or her agenda also have to be noted as part of the

15

process. The advice and guidance process must have the future worker at its core, and be linked to the realities of the markets and opportunities as well as to the person.

A career counsellor needs to be informed about his or her own personal constructs, so that false ideas and aspirations are not projected into the client. He or she must avoid projecting any of their own unfilled ambitions into the worker. For some people this then replicates the parental ambitions which may have been projected into the counsellor – these are unreal, and so cannot be fulfilled at any level by the worker. An awareness of his or her internal worlds is key to the career counsellor, if only to avoid constructing a narcissistic version of themselves in the guise of the worker seeking advice or support. The ways in which the counsellor relates to and perceives the worker are important, and the needs and motivations of both need to be clearly distinct and separate. This may be assumed to be so in an adult relationship in the work environment, but there is a responsibility for the career counsellor to enable the worker to develop in relation to his or her own agenda, and to be an independent person. Any deep-seated need to infantilize the worker, giving the counsellor more imagined power, has to be taken into account.

A competent career support person, able to analyse need and also be aware of the constant contextual changes, can enable a worker to undertake an analysis of personal history and emotions at a suitable level, in order to enable choices to be made from a more informed base. A rigorous and informed approach, supported by efficient information is important. Any distortion of reality or collusion over some elements of the agenda merely produces more discontent. In turn the worker projects anger about all his or her unfilled ideas and phantasies into the world of work, and becomes increasingly disenchanted and bitter. This is then projected into the specific workplace, at other workers and at the counsellor. There is also a need for the counsellor to try and analyse some of the phantasies which workers may bring to them, and not to collude with inappropriate or unrealistic projections. This may be seductive at some level, but prevents real work taking place.

External events and processes also play their part in this interaction. The technologies, with their possibilities and their limitations, plus possible bias in available information, also play key roles in determining the career choice. The updating and maintenance of an information system, as well as its design, will also have an influence on choice, including the degree of interaction and collaboration with the worker. Information literacy is important to both parties, regardless of the format and presentation of the material. Values, possibilities and assumptions need to be explored in relation to reality, rather than to a set of unrealistic ideals, rooted in personal myth and need. Some of the support and, more particularly, some of the literature can be of a superficial nature, and so will not enable genuine personal choices and then development to take place. Information evaluation is crucial, combined with a knowledge of the subject areas. External drivers will affect the content, presentation and ethos of some information. In addition, not all information is necessarily available in hard copy or on-line, and personal recruiting through formal and informal networks is subject to the same distortions involved in all relationships – phantasy, rivalry, anger, the need to control, ambition and many other emotions. The role, identity and effectiveness of the career counsellor can be key to this area of development, and to exploring the complex ideas, relationships and information processing involved.

Personal definition takes time to achieve, and has to be part of a wider personal development, in which work plays a major part. It also has to be synchronous with the growth and emotional maturity of the individual, and cannot be imposed by any external person or force. Psychodynamic thinking may helpfully inform the career counsellor and the worker, and maintain a process of support within a strong framework, but without being intrusive or straying into the complex realms of psychoanalytic analysis.

2 Work: change and the information professional

Rosemary Raddon

... the impulses of conservatism – to ignore or avoid events which do not match our understanding, to control deviation from expected behaviour, to isolate innovation and sustain the segregation of difference aspects of life – are all means to defend our ability to make sense of life. Even if we are wise enough to give up these defences when they become untenable, we still depend on the continuity of conceptions and purposes whose stability as organising structures bring novelty within the grasp of our understanding. Given that this context of meaning is founded at the beginning of life, and develops from the first through relationships with adults whose experience is formed by the society in which they grew up, the meanings we discover must be, in part, those that our parents discovered before us. The continuity of this context represents for an individual his identity; for a society its cultures; and for mankind, perhaps, the half-hidden outline of a universal philosophy. It is necessarily conservative in the sense that it can only change by reformulation. Whatever happens, the continuity of past and present must be preserved; and to revise the principles by which we have interpreted the past is a far more arduous and impenetrable task that to make what happens now conform to them.

(P. Marris (1986) *Loss and Change*, London: Routledge and Kegan Paul, p. 11)

CONTEXT

Having considered the changing and uncertain world of work in its widest context, it is important and also logical to consider the more specific (but equally rapidly changing) world of the information worker. Both these worlds have to be understood, in addition to the ways in which they interrelate with each other, in order to enable career development to take place. The understanding of this interrelationship is key to development, and can be achieved through analysis, communication, contextual understanding, and a willingness to be adaptable and flexible. The relationships, tensions, debates and predicaments between the changing world of the employer and the changing world of the worker are then able to be interpreted and correlated and so more clearly linked to strategies and developments. Career opportunities and development will also change, in conjunction with changing skills and attributes. These skills and attributes have to be managed and actively pursued. This chapter focuses on the context of change, organizational dynamics, professional changes, and the analysis of the person and the professional within this change.

Many external and organizational changes are familiar, but sometimes are seen as distant and unrelated to self, or so close that they are threatening, and so are negated or denied. These changes are reflected in the professional literature, but are not necessarily linked to work in the personal ownership and development sense, or to career progression. Change at policy and strategy levels can easily outstrip change at personal levels, and so create acute dissonance. Such changes can then be distanced, and so any potential sense of threat averted. Awareness of opportunity, of the relationship between opportunity and personal concepts and ambitions, the need for flexibility, for transferable skills, the need to progress some weaker areas of competence, to be clear about the self and the individual place in the professional world – these are all part of the informed analysis of change.

The internal self has its own needs and agenda, and these have to be matched in turn by the external world of work. The world of work has to be supportive, important and relevant to the individual. The reverse means that work is just a method of survival, and the place of work a complex arena of angry and frustrated emotions. Such emotions affect worker and workplace and become destructive. The individual relationship between information professional and the context or organization in which he or she works forms the foundation of a career and career development. This relationship, like all others, functions at a private and unconscious level, as well as at a public and conscious level. The external manifestation of internal issues indicates the complexity of the underlying internal processes. The outward result is the means of perceiving, understanding and managing some of the underlying emotions. The choice of profession, work and place of work is the bedrock on which development grows – choices may be clear for some but not for others. The choices are in themselves important, as they represent future status, or financial independence, achieving recognition, seeking approval, validating deeply held beliefs, or other emotions. Career choice also represents adulthood, the loss of childhood and few responsibilities, and the taking on of a new set of relationships with the new world of work.

ORGANIZATIONAL CHANGES AND DYNAMICS

Organizations are a key element in the process of career development, and can affect decisions which workers may make about their careers. The organizational culture can be absorbed and distort individual thinking and perceptions. For example, some organizations present themselves as very defensive and resistant to change. This is frequently a result of workers erecting psychological barriers to change when they are feeling particularly vulnerable; such defences protect them from these feelings. These are all acted out as a result of internal unconscious confusions, but the result provides external evidence of the internal feelings. Reducing and alleviating the collective anxiety can produce creativity which has been deeply hidden. Managers have a considerable role in this. Strong resistance feelings can be internalized and negate individual ambitions. Anyone working in such organizations and trying to further career development needs to understand this resistance, and to form relationships which allow access to and then exploration of these defences.

In such circumstances, workers may decide to utilize formal support structures, or to look for alternative support, such as informal and semi-social groupings. These support bases may be useful, but can also be used to act as a base from which to constantly attack the organization – such tactics provide immediate satisfaction, but not longer-term solutions. The organization itself may also collude with negative processes. For example, it is possible for the careers adviser or human resource adviser to be seduced into thinking that change is not possible, through his or her unconscious collusion with these collective defences. This then prevents positive work taking place. It is also important that workers are allowed to be creative in support relationships, and so enjoy work. This helps to break down barriers between work and 'other', and prevents a destructive split in living.

Resistance to change can also stem from anger, hostility and the need to hold on to these feelings. They then provide a protection against any disappointment, and can be used to perpetuate the narrative of not achieving or moving on. Others may not wish to work with any kind of support person or mechanism as this would involve a close relationship, and so be perceived as high risk. It may also produce some kind of change, which in itself would be frightening, and so the worker 'kills off' any kind of relationship or change before it is allowed to happen.

Other organizations have opposite patterns, and are in a constant state of change. This is another unconscious way of preventing growth, but the perception of those involved is that change is in fact growth. Constant reorganization then becomes a paradox in which all energies are channelled into change and supporting it. Some information workers may find this useful or opportunistic, but such a process has a negative side, as there is no time to achieve any perceived change before another reorganization takes place. For many workers there is a sense of not having an 'end product'.

It is possible for organizations to generate a constant sense of change through getting rid of elements which are uncomfortable, under the guise of providing new services or systems. So those aspects of the whole which are not really integrated are split off into other areas. This too is unsettling for the workers, as well as for the consumers. Other examples of organizational patterns which are not conducive to good personal and career development are those where relationships are formalized to an extreme extent (titles and role titles used formally, as well as very rigid decision-making structures), or those where responsibilities are avoided or constantly referred to a higher layer of management. This has been perfected in some organizations, but prevents individuals taking any responsibility for themselves. Workers then become dependent, and unwilling to make major career choices or changes. Careers become static and contingent. The opposite pattern is characterized by over-familiarity, with weak or non-existent boundaries, and this too prevents clear decision making in relation to careers.

Some organizations have invested time and energy and money in trying to develop their workforce, and in understanding the results of the interaction between policies, services and workers. The concept of the 'learning organization' is no longer innovative, and the title is merely a development of those places and people who can and do utilize change and growth, working from a position of personal strength and understanding. Stability, in the emotional sense, in such organizations or groups comes from constant exploration and consideration. Knowledge management and the development of strategic roles for library and information services (LIS) professionals flourish in such environments. The use of slick labels and slogans to hide difficult attitudes and behaviours will not achieve stability, and can be a seductive cover-up for underlying illness. The processing, understanding and use of all these interrelationships is outlined in this chapter. Further exploration of the issues follows in Chapter 7 by Rossana Kendall, in Chapter 8 by Liz Roberts, and in addition there are examples of personal changes in the case studies at the end of the book.

LIS CHANGES AND DYNAMICS

Any changes always have to be seen in context. Major issues around the concept of work have already been considered in Chapter 1. As part of this contextual setting, more specific changes in the world of work which affect the LIS professions can be identified, and are considered in this chapter and later in Chapter 5. These changes have an effect on organizations, support mechanisms, and on relationships and growth. They include, for example, change and action as a result of a range of external drivers, involving government directives, profit margins, capitalist philosophies, political agendas, the use of organizations as political stages, technology, and major social and legislative changes. In addition, change is derived from the internal processes of individual workers, indicated by external behaviours. These two elements of professional and wider change constantly interact with each other and with workers. Demands by employers are also in a constant state of change and reinterpretation, driven usually by some of the factors outlined in Chapter 1. These demands, expectations and identified attributes are explored in more detail by Angela Abell in Chapter 5. Other, and differing, attitudes to change are explored by Liz Roberts in Chapter 8. They are all part of the rapid process of change in the LIS as well as other professions.

As part of these changes, organizations need to be aware of anxieties and concerns which stem from workers' fundamental anxieties, and which will in turn affect the functioning of the organization. These are basic and primitive anxieties linked to the need for security, finance and continuity, as identified by Maslow in his 'hierarchy of needs' (Maslow, 1954). The very nature of the work can also cause great anxieties, often demonstrated by those working in the technological, political or financial arenas. Individual personal anxieties can come to the surface and distort patterns of work.

Within this wide arena, the LIS professions are in a state of great change, but changes also provide exciting opportunities. Even the spectre of unemployment can sometimes be used as a period to take stock of work, of personal issues, and of what is priority in the personal context. Unemployment is always a possibility, as within the broader social and economic picture, it is clear that there will always be a segment of the population that is unemployed, and that this may sometimes be used as a focus for other economic and political agendas. However, within the context of the changes outlined in the first chapter, and with increasing stress being laid on the development and exploitation of the technologies, there is also an increasing focus on specific skills shortages. Workers in the LIS professions could utilize some of these shortages to enhance individual portfolios, to change direction, or to move into different sectors. In addition, the increasing stress on the service sector, in its widest sense, may be seen as an opportunity not only to improve the performance of some LIS services, but also to open up new areas of work for those concerned with a range of service deliveries. Markets will open up as a result of increasing market integration, and quality and innovation will be increasingly valued. The universal uses of information, interrelatedness at national and international levels and the increasingly accepted concept of information or knowledge management opens many doors. Current advances in digital preservation and information visualization are examples of far-reaching changes in the applications of technology to the creative use of storage, display and the interrelationships of information. The concept of intellectual capital and its utilization provides LIS opportunities. Accelerated changes in structure, patterns of working, including homeworking using the technologies, will open up opportunities for LIS workers. Linked political connotations, and the management and uses of information in the global context, also provide opportunities.

The technologies of course offer an ever increasing range of opportunities for career initiative and change. The People's Network in the public sector is one example, as is the PULMAN project (Public Libraries Mobilising Advanced Networks), and the National Electronic Library for Health. In addition, social inclusion initiatives also utilize other mechanisms, such as the DCMS/Wolfson Public Libraries Challenge Fund.[1]

Overall, the increasingly clearer identification of skills by employers, and curriculum changes which seek to address these, are all part of major changes. This clearer identification of skills and attributes supports career development and can be harnessed by LIS workers. Communication skills, team working, political awareness, financial awareness, motivation and flexibility will increasingly be in demand by employers. All provide opportunities to move into developing areas such as the voluntary sector, the NHS, marketing, publicity and education, among others. Information professionals can use these changes to move into previously unexplored areas, through demonstrating their acquisition of defined skills and attributes, and responding to employers' needs. As already indicated, the identification of these is explored in Chapter 5 by Angela Abell.

A change of career for the information worker relates to and stems from some or all of these developments. The extent of involvement and change will correlate with the individual agenda, including the extent of self-knowledge, sensitivity, motivation, personal circumstances, drive, enthusiasm, and a commitment to a cause or causes. It may also be a reverse change, when a clear decision is made to opt out of any professional growth process, and to invest in other areas of life. This too has its roots in earlier experiences, and needs to be clearly articulated so that such workers are not perceived as negative. As mentioned, further reflection on this differing expression of individual thinking is explored in more detail in Chapter 8 by Liz Roberts.

Support mechanisms for career development also have to operate within a climate of change. Organizations, structures, networks and individual systems will be affected by change and by personalities, and so this will in turn affect the service or support offered. The places, systems and people which provide career help also have to be seen in context.

Career choice and development has also widened for the informational professional. Part of this has been the rapid change from a print-based and sector-specific profession, to a wider range of skills and contexts, and this is a change which is accelerating. It is acknowledged clearly in the latest report from the Department for Culture Media and Sport, which refers to the access to digital skills as a key element particularly in the development of the public sector (DCMS, 2003). The concept of the knowledge-based economy is now prevalent, and the way in which this is determined and established will provide both opportunities and difficulties for the information worker and for those organizations involved in such changes. Lifelong learning, e-learning and access to the virtual environment to support individuals and communities all provide more opportunities for the LIS worker, as well as key changes in information access within specific growth sectors. Schemes have been devised which create a virtual environment within the public sector, including access to a range of materials through digitization programmes; the Learning for All initiative[2] and the Wider Information and Library Issues Project[3] are examples of developing initiatives. These changes have key sociological and economic implications for those usually excluded from such developments, and particularly for those with physical disabilities. The information worker is at the heart of these changes, but change is difficult and uncomfortable, and unless it is embraced, then career development in the future will be focused within a different, less exciting and more marginalized profession. The Report of the competitiveness and Knowledge-based Economy Executive Advisory Group to CILIP[4] summarizes this well:

> CILIP should develop a skills framework which reflects an information skills continuum, the context of the application of those skills, and a range of skills which enables effective application.
>
> (CILIP..., 2003, p. 7)

The professional changes inevitably include the rapid applications of technology, echoing changes at global level. But these changes are tools, not concepts, and have to be managed and adapted as tools. The resultant changes in policies, organizations, structures, job descriptions and service delivery use the technology to provide more effective and efficient services. The virtual environment, the pervasive use of the Internet and increasing access in the education sector are having huge effects on the information professions. Technology in the primary school determines a generation of students at secondary school, as well as in further and higher education, with high expectations of technology both within and without organizations, and with actual and potential highly sophisticated levels of information literacy. There are enormous implications for information professionals in relation to increasingly sophisticated users as well as in the training of specialist end-users. The debate on education for information professionals is not appropriate here, but is pertinent to the wider picture of the future of the professions.

Barriers are also beginning to break down between the various sectors, as the technology is adopted, and as the glass box or silo concept of service delivery begins (even if sometimes slowly), to break down. The focus on the customer negates the concept of strict boundaries and ownership in the traditional sense, and the increasing access to information sources by the customer adds to the impetus. Technological cooperation is serious in this context, and new schemes, such as the Collaborative Digital Reference Service provided by the Library of Congress, indicate this. Another example in the UK is the 'Gathering the Jewels' digitization programme covering Welsh artefacts.[5] The management of digital content will continue to have considerable implications for the profession. Again there are linked issues relating to the impact of the wider realities of social inclusion and exclusion, and the effects of social and economic marginalization on access to technologies and information.

These changes can be threatening to the known balance of work, but have to go hand in hand with infrastructure changes, management changes, creativity and working across boundaries, all of which help support and develop the individual and provide an increasing range of opportunities. Learning is a key element, for organizations, authorities and individuals. Part of this process is knowing about the self and, with this knowledge, being more able to learn, to share and to take risks. Taking risks involves being more business-orientated, developing business skills, being able to communicate with a wider range of stakeholders, being able to identify and grasp opportunities, and being able to use relevant processes to enhance the changing economy. Business intelligence activities will continue to develop.

Overall, the technologies support and, in some places, drive change. There are, of course, implications here for the information professional, and a need to recognize the concept of easy access by the user in relation to the technologies. There are also implications for career development, as other professions become increasingly aware and competent in the use of the technologies and particularly the information technologies. However it is still true that the provision of sophisticated information systems utilizes at different levels the core skills of classification and indexing (Thesaurus construction and indexing). It is vital that these sophisticated core skills are more effectively exploited in organizational structures by information professionals. There is also in general an increasingly mobile workforce, and an increasingly complex and varied range of workplaces in which the information professional can operate. This offers career flexibility and opportunity. Within these workplaces the sharing of information is crucial, and operates at intra and inter organizational levels. Again this offers career opportunities for those who are able to demonstrate their ability to lead, innovate or contribute to multi-disciplinary teams. Workplaces and organizations are also constantly changing – merging, becoming flatter, outsourcing, linking or operating from other parts of the globe – all these changes can be perceived to be opportunistic for the professional.

Knowledge management is partly a response to some of the global changes outlined earlier, and also to the linked changes in organizational strategies, management structures and systems, all reflecting the changing markets. Technology, and the convergence of some of the technologies, is of course one of the major drivers, and e-commerce and e-business the means to satisfy stakeholders and customers. The considerable literature on the much-debated issue of knowledge management is an indication of the tensions and developments within this area. It is, however, important to recognize the interrelatedness of the defined drivers and the changes they produce, and the changes which are derived from other social and political values. For example, the radical political shifts experienced since the Second World War have made a massive contribution to change, and to social and economic expectations. These expectations have to be satisfied at some level, and so management and technological changes inform and fuel these expectations. The connections at a global level, using the technologies, are reflected at an increasingly sophisticated rate in organizations and networks. Such connections, which may be technologically highly developed, but also based on delicate interpersonal team work, are at the core of knowledge management.

Once some of the language of knowledge management is deconstructed, it can be seen that this is a rapidly changing area, not only in its nomenclature, but in the support, opportunities and excitement that it can offer to the information professional. These opportunities can range from managing a basic information service to becoming, for example, a knowledge manager or knowledge navigator, or other professional. Such posts range from very high to standard salaries, depending on the level of expertise required. Knowledge management also clearly indicates the interrelatedness of disciplines and professions, all utilizing the technology, but requiring also other identifiable skills and attributes, as indicated in Chapter 5 by Angela Abell. The sophistication of this information sharing and access relates to need and context. Key to all this is the provision of information through policies, strategies, standards, services and technologies to respond to a specific need at a specific time. The fluidity of the context and the range of changing roles and jobs add to the opportunities as organizations change and develop. Career development can thrive in such a context of change and shifting boundaries. Sensitivity, innovation, flair, collaboration, intellectual linking and imagination, allied to appropriate technical skills, will all help the aspiring information professional to move forward.

The essence of change and the requisite skills, abilities and attributes to support change have been considered and written about since the information professions first began searching for an adequate label, and reflect those dilemmas that employers have been grappling with for an equally long time. Many of the core concepts have changed in nomenclature, but in concept have widened, rather than changed radically. For example, the Confederation of British Industry (1998) tried to synthesize the needs of employers, which included interpersonal skills, management skills, technical abilities, team working, political skills and communication skills. These attributes are also identified each year by employers looking for graduates from the university sector, and also include strategic thinking, risk taking and the enjoyment of the challenge of change. These attributes could in turn be rewritten using other descriptors, but are in essence clearly related to those identified as being core to knowledge management environments. These have been refined to include interpersonal skills, team working, advanced technological skills, planning skills, business understanding and the ability to be able to contribute to the knowledge base. Any information professional will be able to, and must, identify, develop and adapt these to suit his or her individual career pattern in relation to changing contexts. The levels of achievement will of course have to correlate to individual needs and personality, but need to be flexible as required by expectation and ambition. Achievement also relates to market needs and the reformatting of individual skills and competencies.

The basis of development and growth is generated by the core attributes of the informational professional. Career planning skills are needed to underpin these, and support personal aims. Such support is available through the workplace, through professional networks and support groups, and specialist agencies and personnel. Career guidance services, psychometric testing, personal counselling, and specialist workplace support are all part of career planning and development. Careful utilization of all these mechanisms, linked to self-awareness, can help to ensure that employability is maintained, through flexibility, utilizing change and maximizing the concept of lifelong learning.

FITTING WORKER AND WORK – QUESTIONING THE PROCESS OF CHANGE

Having considered work, its context, importance and changes, the next logical step is to consider how the individual relates to the organization or setting in which he or she functions. This is to ensure the 'fit' between worker and working context, to provide maximum satisfaction. This fit has to accommodate the external reality of available opportunities and conditions, and the internal processes and feelings. This relationship involves some considerable degree of self-assessment in order to be able to answer such fundamental questions such as, 'why am I here?', 'what am I doing here?' and 'where else could I or do I want to be?'. There is a need to be able to function and develop from an informed position, rather than by being driven – not a revolutionary concept, but many workers are caught up in a cycle or cycles which they are unable to break but which are not satisfying or fulfilling. There may be a sense of being out of control, but unable to determine why or when this sense arose. Feeling that there is not a fit between self and work can be overwhelming and confusing, leading to confusion and anger in other areas of the worker's life. The underlying anger or depression has to be dealt with, often by projecting these emotions into the place of work, the managers, fellow workers or family and friends. However, understanding why those cycles are interesting or appealing in the first place, why and how one is caught up in them, and how they attract both one's conscious and unconscious thoughts, enable clearer and so more satisfying decisions to be made about work and career.

Some of the personal questions which need to be addressed as part of the career process could include:

- Why am I in this job at this time?
- What are the positive and negative factors?
- How much satisfaction am I getting from work?
- Am I demonstrating my skills and competencies?
- Am I demonstrating my attributes?
- Where do I want to be?
- Why do I want to be there?
- What do I need to get there?
- How do I fill any gaps in my skills and experience portfolio to get there?
- What support mechanisms do I have?
- How much time and effort am I prepared to invest in the career process?
- How well do I know myself?
- How well do I want to know myself?
- What are my strongest qualities?
- What are my weakest characteristics?
- How and where do I function most effectively?

And last, but not least:

- Am I still growing and developing?
- Is the balance of my life satisfactory?
- Where is the dissonance (if any)?
- Do the internal (the private or unconscious self) and external (the public or work self) elements of life support and enhance each other?

These may appear to be relatively straightforward questions, but if addressed and thought about honestly, can contribute to the compilation of a relatively accurate personal profile in relation to work. Even the process of responding to the questions – genuinely responding to them, distorting the responses a little, or being economical with the truth – can help contribute to the profile if this process is also considered. Sensitive areas can be explored, as well as the reasons for their sensitivity. Areas that appear to be satisfactory can also be explored further – are these really satisfactory and integrated areas of the self, or are defence mechanisms used to hide other difficulties? It can be useful to repeat this questioning process on an annual basis, or when work changes, to ensure that personal development is kept up to date. This enables the worker to enhance areas that can contribute to career development, and to be aware of personal growth.

To make a more coherent and informed 'fit' between work and self involves an analysis of the workplace, in the context of the changes outlined in the earlier chapter, and an analysis of the 'whole' person. This can be as sophisticated or as basic as need and interest determine. There have been many theorists writing in the area of exploring the inner world in relation to external actions and emotions, including of course Freud (1986), Jung (Storr, 1983), Klein (1987), Winnicott (1965), Bowlby (1975) and many others. Jung's writing on the aspects of life which give meaning to the persona form a key element in the debate. The concept of 'wholeness', as defined by Jung, is key to the development of self as well as career.

> If the unconscious can be recognised as a co-determining factor along with consciousness, and if we can live in such a way that conscious and unconscious demands are taken into account as far as possible, then the centre of gravity of the total personality shifts its position. It is then no longer in the ego, which is merely the centre of consciousness, but in the hypothetical point between conscious and unconscious. This new centre might be called the self.
>
> (Jung, 1983, p. 19)

Some of these concepts have been used in the development of management theories, and in personal development. The literature is considerable and clearly applicable to the concept of career development and the relationships between individuals and organizations. It also includes the work of Kets de Vries (1995), Menzies (1970) and Hirschhorn (1990), referred to later in Chapter 6 by Rossana Kendall, as well as de Board (1978). The concept of being creative, including being creative at work, was also explored by Maslow (1994) but tends to be an element of his writing that is often overlooked. He felt that the unifying effects of balancing or accepting the inner and outer worlds of the persona led to greater creativity in all areas of life, and that this included the work context.

> My feeling is that the concept of creativeness and the concept of the healthy, self-actualizing, fully human person seem to be coming closer and closer together and may perhaps turn out to be the same thing.

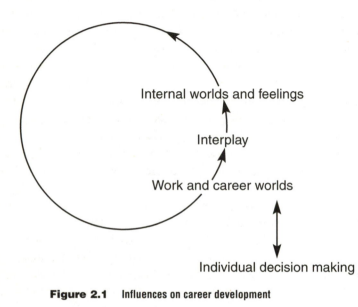

Figure 2.1   Influences on career development

There are many ways in which such a personal analysis or overview can be carried out, and these can be used in ways needed and so determined by the individual. All must be taken in context and within their own limitations, as no support system is perfect or applicable to everyone all of the time. Some may be used for a short time, others for longer periods, some in isolation, others in conjunction with each other on the traditional 'need to know' basis. However, it is useful to consider how to achieve a closer relationship and fit between worker and work, and this is explored through a consideration of some of these tools in the next chapter. Career development then becomes more coherent and cohesive if the internal and external worlds of the individual are synchronized around known and understood key issues. It is also important to note that change and ambition can be linked to phantasy and narcissism. The illusion of change and development may be strong, but may remain an illusion. Reality becomes harder to accept and so phantasy and abstract ideas become much easier to cope with – they act as an escape mechanism. As indicated, the next chapter focuses on and explores overt ways in which preparations for change can lead into the actual management of change. These preparations have their own dynamics, but again can be used as vital personal development, identifying what can be achieved by an individual, and exploring some difficult areas of personal growth.

NOTES

1   For further information on the organizations mentioned in this paragraph see the following websites:
    People's Network: http://www.peoplesnetwork.gov.uk
    PULMAN Project: http://www.pulmanweb.org
    National Electronic Library for Health: http://www.nelh.nhs.uk
    DCMS Wolfson Grant Programme: http://www.culture.gov.uk/heritage/wolfson
2   For further information on Learning for All see: http://www.learndirect.co.uk/
3   For further information on the Wider Information and Library Issues Project see: http://www.resource.gov.uk/
4   This report is also available at: http://www.cilip.org.uk/advocacy/eags/keagreport.html
5   See: http://www.gtj.org.uk

3 Preparation for change: support mechanisms, dynamics and processes

Rosemary Raddon

Every individual has the responsibility to reassess the satisfaction and pleasures derived from career and personal life. This suggestion implies a reduction of self-indulgence, the opportunity to express feelings about personal life and career, the willingness to engage in mutual problem solving, and a sense of generativity towards the young management generation. These matters become important for both individual and organization, and will enable the executive to traverse the quicksand which can be mid-career, and make it a station on the route to personal growth and generativity, instead of the marking point of decline.

(M.F.R. Kets de Vries (1995), *Organizational Paradoxes: Clinical Approaches to Management.* 2nd edn, London: Routledge and Kegan Paul, p. 158)

INTRODUCTION

A clearer perspective on some of the support mechanisms which help the individual can act as a foundation for development and change. Such mechanisms or support processes can provide a springboard for the next post, promotion, or a move into different areas of work. They also generate their own dynamics, which are explored in the second half of this chapter. The individual person can utilize such programmes in a way that is appropriate to the context in which he or she works.

An analysis of the work context and of the ways in which the worker can be supported within this enable a clearer relationship to be established between the two components – of work and the associated career development. This analysis also enables the worker to perceive the changing tensions, structures, boundaries, power centres, limitations and intensity of support within his or her world. A clearer perspective of the available approaches and structures enables a much more informed choice to be made about if, what, where and how career development can take place.

This perspective can then complement an increased awareness of the individual personal arena. The interlinking of work, support mechanisms and the self become more transparent and manageable.

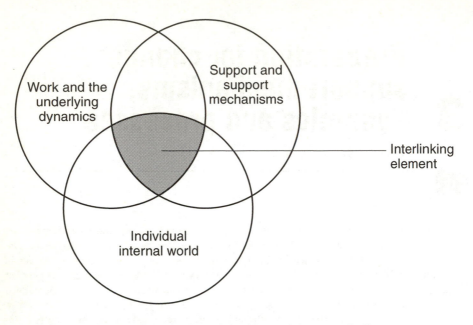

Figure 3.1 Core relationship – work, support and self

Understanding and utilizing as many as possible of these interrelated forces comprise one of the major elements in the process of choosing, managing and developing a career. The choices involved are at the heart of all career growth, decision making and development. Choice springs from being informed, and so from taking control of events rather than being controlled by them. From choice and increased security grows the ability to sustain awareness, identify what is available and where, process relevant information, manage it, and sustain growth and change. The case studies also illustrate some of the dynamics of these areas.

SUPPORT MECHANISMS

PSYCHOMETRIC AND PERSONALITY ASSESSMENT

The use of psychometric testing is one major area which can be helpful in assessing or profiling the individual. There are many tests available today, but one which is used frequently in the workplace is Myers-Briggs (Myers, 1993). The concepts used are derived from the work of Jung. It is, however, as its name implies – Myers-Briggs Type Indicator – an indicator only, and the indicators change in relation to the worker's life, external issues and circumstances. It is an instrument which represents the individual's response in the external or conscious world, to his or her unconscious drives. The choices and decisions which are made as a result of this identified orientation are consistent with the internal persona. The indicator can thus help in the understanding of differing personalities, and so enable problems, tasks and the workplace to be fitted more comfortably to the individual and to teams. The indicator can also provide a valid and personal foundation for development, and help find and support a sense of direction. It illustrates the way in which a person relates to the world with their own individual styles and preferences. The test reduces these relationships and preferences to a set of four descriptors, using indicative capital letters.

The test has been measured over many years to check if it does indeed measure what it is intended to measure, using tests related to content validity, construct validity and criterion validity. The concept is based on the use by everyone of four basic functions or processes which determine actions; in addition there are two major but differing attitudes which determine lifestyles. Two other major preferences also indicate personal operating styles. The functions, attitudes and preferences then provide a framework of personality types. The resultant descriptors can be used with individuals to explore areas of tension, reduce stress, provide a basis for personal development and clearly link personality with relevant or satisfying work patterns.

The two major processes and preferences are related to energy, and the source of personal energy. This can be derived from the external world, such as other people and work, or from the inner world of thoughts and feelings. These are described respectively as extroversion and introversion. They are ways of relating to the world, and so they determine general lifestyles and the general use of the preferred functions. The extroverted preference indicates an individual mainly reliant on the external world, on other people or events, to provide stimulation, and the energy to change. The introverted attitude is not the social concept of introversion, but one in which the individual draws energy from an inner world of ideas. Such individuals tend to be concerned with long-term ideas and concepts, and do not necessarily have to be part of a wider group of people.

The information-processing elements of life are grouped under two labels – sensing and intuition. Sensing can be applied to realists who are very much caught up in 'the moment', who make decisions and function through reality and evidence. Intuition can be applied to those who process and make decisions through insight, relationships, making connections and possibilities and following innate intuition. This preference is often concerned with future ideas and plans rather than with the reality of the present. They are preferences which indicate tension in approaches.

The decision-making elements of life are grouped under another two linked preferences. These are labelled as thinking and feeling. Those who prefer the thinking element operate using information, facts and ways of processing observations. On the other hand, those whose preference is for the feeling indicator make decisions linked to their own feelings, their concern for others, and their own values.

Other preferences relate to the indicators which can be used to illustrate ways in which the individual conducts his or her life at a personal level. Judgement and perception are the two major indicators which indicate styles of living and organizing. Judgement indicates a more structured way of operating, with clear organizational boundaries, using information, making clear decisions, and being clear about decision making. The perception preference indicates a way of life which is more flexible, more intuitive, open to new experiences and ideas, and which enjoys concepts and exploration.

Through completing a questionnaire, individuals can then see their own preferences, indicated as capital letters for each of the preferences. So an individual may be identified, as 'ENTP', showing that energy is derived from others – extrovert. The chosen lifestyle is perceptive, and attention is paid to intuition and the ideas attached to this. Thinking relates to the chosen style of decision making. Seen as a 'snapshot', this personal assessment can be very productive in illustrating major elements in the persona, and those that may need developing, as well as others which may need more care. The process can be related to the workplace, to relationships, or to developmental activities and career development. It can also indicate personal areas which may need to be further developed to give a more balanced persona in order to achieve this closer relationship or understanding between work and the worker.

Myers-Briggs has been used as a basis for a considerable amount of work in this area, and the concepts have been developed to support a range of tests and inventories. A recent example is the *Personality Survey System* devised by Success Dynamics International Ltd (2003),[1] which uses descriptors such as honesty, courage, etc.: many others are available on the Internet. The use of such devices is another indication of changes in employment and reflects the need to provide employers with a tangible indication of some personal attributes, development and growth by employees.

OTHER TESTS AND INDICATORS

The Myers-Briggs Type Indicator is only one of a range of psychological assessment instruments, but is probably one of the most popular and widely used. Others include the California Psychological Inventory, the Kolb Learning Style Inventory, the Adjective Checklist and the Minnesota Multiphasic Personality Inventory. The FIRO-B is another instrument that evaluates interpersonal needs and behaviour. The Five Factor test, used by occupational psychologists, is also widely used to try and relate individuals to specific jobs, and to identify individual personality traits. Specific aptitude tests are also used to check on the level of skills displayed by workers in relation to particular jobs. They are also used to indicate the ability of workers to learn and change and adapt in relation to particular circumstances. The Aptitude for Business Learning Exercises (ABLE) is an example of a test used to assess skills within a work context.

In all cases, the efficacy of such indictors relates in part to the person administrating and analysing the results, with all the inbuilt prejudices that this implies. Most tests tend to be Euro-centric, and some have had a gender bias. However, in relation to managing cultural diversity, psychometric tests are now being developed to try and overcome obstacles related to gender and race, which have had adverse impacts on the person and the workplace. They are also being developed to make them more accessible for people with visual or other impairments.

In addition to psychometric and personality testing, there are other support strategies and techniques which support the individual in his or her career development. As with so many issues in the area of growth and personal progression, many of these overlap with each other and with other organizational issues. It is, however, possible to distinguish some clear strands and to identify broad characteristics and techniques which support the individual. Some of these strategies can be used in a 'stand alone' situation, while others may be used in conjunction with other support mechanisms, tests or management processes.

MENTORING

Another support process is mentoring. This is in essence very similar to coaching, but is much more focused on the advice and encouragement given by a very experienced person to a less experienced person, based in the workplace. Advice, encouragement and support are the main elements of the process, based on a one-to-one relationship. One definition of mentoring is that it

> incorporates a variety of different approaches with this in common: a focus on a one-to-one relationship between mentor and learner which ensures individual attention and support for the learner.

> (Corrall, 1994, cited by Nankivell, 2000)

Mentoring is frequently and more generally used in the workplace, but is also used in further and higher education. In the latter, a mentor such as an experienced or third-year student may be appointed to guide a new student. It can also be used to support students working in more isolated fields, such as research, or to postgraduates.

The specific roles, methods and resources used in mentoring vary enormously, and correspond to the needs of specific individuals and organizations. They include mentors working in the role of adviser, confidante, counsellor, supporter, facilitator and professional support. The mentor needs key skills, including the ability to listen, communicate in a sensitive way, analyse, and also be creative and innovative within the relationship. Conflict resolution may also be an important element.

This strategy of mentoring focuses on the individual, and supports the developmental process and experiential learning. The relationship can be formal or informal, and again a knowledge of the individual persona, of both mentor and mentee, can enhance the relationship. This knowledge can have been gained through management development, counselling, psychometric testing, or any other support mechanism (including the SWOT analysis, for example) which enriches the relationship. It can also help to prevent any misplaced emotions and misunderstandings which arise in a close relationship. There is a clear need to define the purpose of the relationship and the boundaries within the context of the specific organization or setting.

Mentoring, particularly familiar in the corporate and higher education sectors, can provide a key element of support in career development and planning. It can be used to develop general management skills, to enhance career prospects through a wider perspective of the LIS professions, to develop specific skills that are seen to be important or transferable, or to develop a particular aspect of the mentee that has been highlighted as needing to be strengthened. In addition it will be a key element in the CILIP Framework of Qualifications. It has been defined by the Industrial Society[2] as:

> a one-to-one relationship between an individual and a more experienced person who can guide and help them to learn and develop in the organization, including an understanding of the organization's culture. Their relationship is confidential and non-judgemental.
>
> (Industrial Society, 1996, p. 1)

A mentor can be from the same organization or sector, or someone from a different area but who has sufficient personal status and expertise to enable a viable and supportive relationship to be established. Communication and interpersonal skills are frequently areas which are targeted for development. Mentoring can of course also be used to familiarize a new appointee with an organization or institution, and can use printed and audio-visual material as part of the familiarization process. This will overlap a little with induction, but differs in that one person is clearly identified who will relate to the new appointee. The relationship is a crucial element within the induction process.

In addition to the ongoing support provided for the mentee, the mentor also benefits from this process. He or she becomes more aware of personal strengths and weaknesses, and also of the need to communicate effectively, and to have a clear vision of the needs of the organization in which both work. LIS professionals can use this strategy for personal development, and can also use expertise from other sectors. This sharing enhances personal growth as well as broadening perspectives – another key transferable attribute.

COACHING

Coaching has grown in popularity in recent years but, like so many other concepts, has emerged from other areas, and embraces a range of philosophies and techniques while at the same time developing its own clear framework. The impetus behind coaching is to help individuals determine what they really want in relation to work and personal life, and to try and determine how this could be achieved. The links to the work of Egan (1998) and Ryle (1990) can be clearly seen, while allowing coaching to be a valid instrument which can stand alone as a support mechanism or tool. The basis of coaching is the facilitation of performance to enhance the individual, the team or the group. As identified by the Industrial Society (1999, p. 3), the overall aim is to improve results through personal effectiveness.

Coaching is about encouraging and supporting learning in an individual, contributing to their performance, and so to the overall work and success of the organization in which they operate. It focuses on utilizing opportunities for development, and allows the learner to explore these at a very personal level. The learner takes responsibility for his or her actions, and can take on initiatives and develop these. It is a proactive process.

Coaching encourages individuals to stand back from external reality, and to try and determine what issues are frustrating or blocking them from achieving what they really want. This requires support and analysis, but focuses on what is preventing achievement at work, or preventing a balance in personal life – it does not try to determine the underlying emotions and feelings or to determine their source. This is the key difference between coaching and counselling – the former is much more concerned with external realities, the latter is more concerned about how internal issues affect and determine these external realities. Coaching provides clear frameworks, and often includes clearly defined goals, and so helps give the individual a strong sense of direction, and of being contained. Clarification of thoughts and feelings which exist in a rather incoherent way can be difficult for an individual caught up in these difficulties, and the coach can help in clearly identifying areas which relate to work, to home or to personal growth. Coaching can help release creativity and reduce anxiety, and put ideas and ambitions into a realistic perspective.

Some coaching relationships are conducted on a personal level, away from the work context (and this may be so if the work environment is problematic), while others may take place at work. Some of the larger corporate companies employ their own coaches, and offer support to all their staff as part of a wider support mechanism. Others use coaches to support senior staff and then, in classical tradition, the ideas can 'trickle down' to those at lower levels in the organization. This concept is then challenged when organizations become flatter, or when the concept of strict hierarchies begins to soften and change. As with any support mechanism, coaching needs to be fully supported by policies, and so implemented throughout any organization. A relationship has to be formed and trusted before it can be fully utilized to help develop an individual, and so cannot be erratic, or seen to be marginal to major areas of work. But if the relationship and the work is allowed to grow, the results can be very positive and rewarding. The individual can then contribute to the overall organization in a more meaningful way, as well as being clearer about his or her own goals.

In the LIS professions there are many opportunities for coaching, as so many organizations are relatively tightly structured, and coaching can be identified as a clear element of management development. Resources are of course an issue, but it is possible to negotiate to share these, so that personal growth can be seen as a part of personal responsibility. It is also possible to develop a more informal approach to coaching, utilizing networks or colleagues in other sectors who are willing to share their expertise. Some individuals pay for individual coaching, as this is seen as a clear investment in self. Decisions on how and where to implement coaching depend on many factors, but personal choice is a strong element. The more experience and knowledge the information professional has of a range of sectors and the issues and developments within them, the easier it then becomes to develop their transferable skills and be ready to take up opportunities when these present themselves.

Through enhancing individual effectiveness, coaching adds to the effectiveness of an organization and improves the motivation of staff. It encourages a clearer look at working practices, and helps prevent work being blamed for personal difficulties and negative attitudes. It encourages the taking on of personal responsibility for development, and of flexibility in attitude. Relationships are improved with increased self-confidence, and this in turn can help to develop existing and potential management skills. Team working is also enhanced through clearer personal objectives and commitment. Coaching also encourages a continuous process of development, and this constant self-regeneration also enhances relationships at the workplace and elsewhere. It can cross boundaries, operate in complex environments, enhance communication processes, increase awareness of political agendas and enhance team skills, A sense of exploration and risk taking can also grow from a coaching situation, giving an enhanced sense of personal responsibility, and this will have an impact on the culture of the organization. This culture is a key element in enabling coaching to have a positive effect. The valuing of learning and change has to be inherent in the management philosophy.

The individual persona of the learner will of course also affect the process and the extent to which this is known or denied. It is possible to be very defensive against change, and to attribute lack of success or fulfilment to the organization, to colleagues, to lack of resources, lack of trust, or other factors. Suspicion of help and support can stem from previous emotional experiences, and so prevent coaching from being effective. A need to be 'told' and contained can also act as a defence, again linking to personal issues. Fear of personal exploration can also prevent a coaching relationship from growing. This is another example of an internal experience, linked to maternal relationships, having a strong effect on external relationships in the workplace.

As in all relationships, success inevitably depends to a large extent on the relationship between the coach and the client. Personalities, style, time, training and previous experiences will all affect the relationship, and so some flexibility and 'shopping around' is important if an individual coach is used. A track record is important to give trust. The relationship is based on sharing, or knowledge, of skills and of experience, and so trust and respect is important. Confidentiality is also important. If the relationship is flawed or uncertain, then the coaching will not be as effective as that generated by a close and trusting relationship. The coach has to allow the learner to develop at his or her own speed, and to take responsibility for individual actions, while not negating his or her own role within the situation – a balance between the two elements is key for success. The coach also has to be detached, flexible, an excellent listener, have authority as well as sensitivity, and be supportive as well as relaxed. His or her training has to be effective, and at the same time enable boundaries to be kept between management and coach. The coach must also be aware of their own personal issues, and how these affect their life and way of operating. This is important as otherwise there is a danger that unconscious issues are played out in the relationship, preventing real progress. If a great deal of acting out takes place, then this activity, unconsciously driven, will be experienced as reality. Any identified plans will then be affected and altered by this different perspective on reality.

It is important to create a climate in which both parties are able to change internally, but the learner also has to want to develop, and to move from a state of not knowing to conscious competence. This development may produce a range of emotions, including anger, frustration, envy and defence. These are all to be expected in the context of such a close relationship, and if the coach is sufficiently in tune with the emotional world, then he or she needs to acknowledge the feelings in the relationship, and allow them to be processed. This will all contribute to the learning process.

In addition to the emotional process, it is equally important that in the context of external reality in the workplace, goals, options, feedback and long-term aims must be clear. They need to be established and agreed by both coach and employee, so that progress can be seen and acknowledged. This assessment process also contributes to personal development in a clear and overt way. The clarity of the process supports and relates to a good working, trusting relationship with commitment on both sides.

PERSONAL COUNSELLING

Counselling can take place within the workplace, or can be an individual and private arrangement. This process is very much concerned with issues which may be difficult to articulate, because of fear, anger, uncertainty, unhappiness or other conflicting emotions. The counselling relationship can explore these feelings and some of the reasons for them, and enable the emotions to be managed at an external level in the workplace. Again this enables career progression, change of career, decision to opt out, or any combination of these, to be clearly externalized from a basis of understanding.

This increasing personal awareness, of self-knowledge, is the opposite of allowing external events to take over or make decisions for individuals, which would then stack up feelings of resentment, anger, and a host of unknown emotions as a result of being driven by unknown forces. Counselling is not about giving advice, but allowing the individual to explore some of the issues which are personal and specific to him or her, within a context of confidentiality. Client expectations, background, needs and possible aims all have to be explored within defined parameters. Bowlby stated:

that one can only understand a person's internal world if one can see how (it) has come to be constructed from the real-life events to which he has been exposed.

(Cited in Holmes, 1993, p. 130)

Again, such increasing self-knowledge leads to increasingly informed decision making. As defined by the BACP (British Association for Counselling and Psychotherapy):

the task of counselling is to give the client an opportunity to explore, discover and clarify means of living more resourcefully and towards greater well-being.

(BACP, 1993)

PEER GROUPS

Career development can also be progressed through peer group support. This process can be organized so that it takes place within or without the workplace, and at a formal or informal level. Regardless of the level of formality of the process, it is important that individuals feel supported, and also that they can discuss strengths and weaknesses in an atmosphere of trust and empowerment. To be able to acknowledge areas of uncertainty and need, and then make decisions on how best to develop and improve them, enhances confidence, and thus performance.

Peer group support can be organized by senior staff, either for themselves or for more junior members of staff, and be formalized within the organizational learning and development structure. The group can then meet within work time, and be integral to personal development. Such support can also be informal, when groups of professionals who share common issues, difficulties and goals arrange to meet regularly. These meetings can be semi-social, and take place in a place convenient and pleasant for all those involved, but while still adhering to strict boundaries of confidentiality and support.

A more sophisticated form of peer group support and individual development can be achieved through involvement in an action learning group. This uses counselling concepts, but within a managerial framework. Action learning is a process which focuses on issues and problem solving at work, within a group context. Through involvement in the group, identifying specific management issues and their approach to these, individuals also develop an awareness of their own strengths and weaknesses. This understanding thus makes a considerable contribution to personal as well as managerial development.

ACTION LEARNING

An action learning group needs to be facilitated by an experienced manager, counsellor or trainer, to meet regularly for at least several hours, and to focus on specific work issues through counselling and questioning mode. It was defined by Revans (1980, p. 309), one of its main protagonists, as '... action learning is about real people tackling real problems in real time ...'. At the end of each session, the group process as a whole is also reviewed, indicating relationships and tensions within the group. Personal issues inevitably arise, and the importance of the facilitator becomes increasingly clear. The discussion on the factors which arise, either managerial or personal, provide the basis for individual development. Confidentiality is key, and the group must learn to support each other and respect individuals, as well as personal and group boundaries. The contract between members of the group, the defining of problems and issues, the respect for individuals and the setting of personal goals are all clearly defined within the concept of action learning. The analysis of issues, taking responsibility for the self, listening and having respect for other members of the group are all elements of personal development. This clarity enhances the potential of such groups for trust and growth.

The identification and analysis of issues important to the individual are key to this process, as these frequently indicate external managerial areas which may be of concern, or cause acute distress or difficulties. These in turn can stem from internal or personal undeveloped areas, such as insecurity, anger, diffidence, or even fear. Identification of any of these barriers to personal growth is the beginning of change. Unresolved and complex parental relationships are frequently acted out in the workplace, and can affect managerial competencies. The workforce is used unconsciously by many people as a mechanism to carry these unresolved emotions, and so contribute to a distortion in achieving policies and service deliveries. Any or all of these issues may need to be developed, in an appropriate way, to cope with the external reality of organizational life, and to personal and career development.

The experiences gained through involvement in such a group over a long period of time not only allow for personal development and career growth, but the symbiotic benefits of understanding more clearly the needs and problems of others in the organization. Managers may become more sensitive to staff, and individuals more aware of issues relating to their peers.

From this basis, managerial tactics and insights may be developed which enhance personal and organizational growth. Analysis, clarification of aims and objectives, establishing tactics, the identification of successful initiatives, reviewing strategies, enhancing performance, improving listening, questioning and facilitating skills are all part of action learning. The strength of action learning lies in developing and facilitating the growth of the individual, but within a learning, not taught, context.

SHADOWING

This is another way of developing personal management and leadership skills, and has some inevitable overlaps with other developmental areas. This does not detract from its value as a way of encouraging growth and personal insights. It involves using opportunities in the workplace to observe and participate in good management practice, to be able to work in another place or situation, and to absorb some of the qualities and skills involved in managerial decision-making practices and procedures. There is a need for both parties to be in full agreement about the shadowing arrangement, and personal communication between both parties is important. This is to ensure that the person shadowing is able to feel comfortable in identifying appropriate areas of service development, but also areas of potential growth and change which could contribute to his or her overall career development and personal awareness.

MANAGERIAL MECHANISMS

Career development can also be supported through formal or organizational managerial mechanisms and systems. The complexity and detail will relate to the individual context, but in all cases there should be clear pre-determined principles utilizing relevant processes. These mechanisms and systems include quality control, performance review, performance assessment, reviews, annual appraisal, peer appraisal, staff audit skills and monitoring. These may be managed as centrally driven programmes or as process-driven programmes, using models such as action learning. All these tools and frameworks, regardless of their nomenclature, are designed to help individuals address areas of personal and professional potential, within a wider framework of improved performance and individual satisfaction in the workplace. They address issues which link people, work and the interaction between the two. Communication processes are also improved. Appraisal processes are very supportive if used correctly, and can help create training programmes, match the needs of the individual with the requirements of the organization, help establish clear goals, and also contribute to equality in the workplace through a structured programme. They can, however, be used in a more behaviourist and less creative way. However, even this more rigid use of such mechanisms can provide support to the worker through the use of the analysis involved, and support professional practice.

All these mechanisms should also help to clearly define both personal and organizational or contextual objectives, to help fit the process of management to individual frameworks. Specific career plans or initiatives should also be included. Individual training and development needs can then be more clearly linked to identified objectives. (These must in turn be specific, measurable, and relate to the long-term aims of the organisation.) Managerial mechanisms, when effective, support both managers and managed.

The culture, scope and general strategies will vary from organization to organization, but all should be seen as positive support mechanisms, rather than threats. They are only one element in the developmental process, and link closely with skills analysis and competency analysis and demand. All in turn are influenced by external politics, economics and technologies. Individuals need to be aware of these changing external drivers.

JOB APPLICATIONS

The process of applying for jobs can also be seen as part of the development of an individual, and can contribute to career planning. The recruitment process can provide valuable feedback to an individual, either at an overt or covert level. The clear identification of required attributes and skills for a particular job, and the matching of these to individual attributes and skills, can pinpoint areas which need attention and development, or those that have been neglected for a range of reasons. The compilation of an application form is also good personal analysis. To be included, or not, on the shortlist is another analytical process. The reasons for not being shortlisted can point to areas of personal and career development which require support. The interview process will test interpersonal and communication skills, as well as other transferable skills, such as time management. Feedback from job interviews is also a valuable contribution to the construction of a personal profile.

RECRUITMENT AGENCIES

Linked to the application process is that of using recruitment agencies to obtain either full- or part-time employment. The application process again very clearly points out areas that are in high demand by employers, and attributes that are considered essential. This gives a basis for personal development using whatever source and mechanism is appropriate. In addition, taking up short-term work can also provide excellent additional experience in other sectors or areas of specialism.

Gender and race may again be issues – ones that are not necessarily openly addressed, but which may raise areas which require personal exploration before addressing in the work arena. The legal requirements for the recruitment process will have to be met, but the hidden agendas are those that will need to be explored. The considerable literature on the subject indicates that male 'models' and male criteria are still very much apparent in the realms of higher management, but an awareness of these is pertinent to individual development. Ways of coping with and overcoming these difficulties must relate to individual circumstances, but have to be acknowledged. Emotional resilience, creativity, motivation, sensitivity, social skills and mental agility are all transferable skills which relate to these areas of difficulty, but which can be utilized in overcoming prejudice. Self-knowledge is again a key part of the process of personal and career development.

SKILLS TOOLKITS

Another element in the process of fitting and developing the self to appropriate organisations or contexts is the use of skills toolkits. These can be used in conjunction with personal development plans to establish areas of potential development. They focus on the analysis of the self, to identify growth and career potential. Some have been developed specifically for the LIS profession, including those being developed by national agencies such as isNTO. The interim publication in 2001 by TFPL on scenario planning (Skelton and Abell, 2001) contained core ideas relating to long-term strategic LIS skills. (TFPL are providers of recruitment, training and consultancy services in the field of knowledge and information management.) Other guides of this nature have been developed within universities, such as that designed for continuing professional development at the University of Central Lancashire (Centre for Research in Library and Information Management, 1997). Toolkits aim to identify a holistic overview of skills, preferences and needs as well as support mechanisms and resources. They are used as individual learning packages or programmes, and feed into the individual's overall development, enhancing personal profiles.

JOB SWAPS

Swapping jobs with another person in a different sector or who utilizes a different set of skills and competencies is a similar concept. Swaps are usually organized for a specific period of time, with a specific contract, and both organizations of course have to agree to the process. So, for example, a person in the public sector may exchange jobs with someone from the corporate sector for a certain period, or work from home, or experience a freelance information agency. Such exchanges have been supported and facilitated by Re:source (now absorbed into the Museums, Libraries and Archives Council), and so are integrating management and development issues into the national framework. Collaborative working is a variant on this process, and involves working professionally, maybe at committee level, or on integrated projects, with personnel from a different sector or area of specialism. Lateral transfers – moving into other departments or sections within the same structure – also broadens experience and widens the skills base. This is a valuable learning experience, and can relate to state-of-the-art technological initiatives, or to different services and provision. Joining or implementing new initiatives in the growth areas of freelance information and knowledge management also provides additional experience and skills. This gives another impetus to the process of change (Hyams, 2002).

PROFESSIONAL DEVELOPMENT PROGRAMMES

Workshops and seminars may be provided within organizational settings or externally, by a range of providers. The professional development programme (chartership) run by the Chartered Institute of Library and Information Professionals may include workshops and seminars, and is a very structured and highly developed professional development process. This structured programme provides feedback and analysis, and so has a relationship with job applications and interviews, as feedback from these also can be used to clearly indicate areas of demand, evidence of weaker areas, or of potential growth. It is important to determine which professional areas need specific support, and to target these and work on them in relation to career plans. Attendance at a 'magic mix' of workshops and seminars will not enhance job applications or support growth. Workshops and seminars may be subject-specific, such as those on business information sources, or linked to transferable skills and attributes, such as technological and managerial competencies. The latter have to be constantly updated to maintain credibility, either through workshops, or through on-the-job training.

Seminars and workshops are also organized on a cross-sectoral basis, and this also gives valuable insights into different policies and practices, which may contribute to movement and career growth across sectors.

COURSES – CAREER ENHANCEMENT

Linked to these are courses which may be at sub-degree, degree or postgraduate level, either full- or part-time, but which can enhance basic qualifications. They can be focused on technical developments, management skills and competencies, human resource development, or related areas such as counselling skills. These can also be supported by training in related areas, such as negotiating and facilitating skills – courses are available at many levels to support specific need and circumstances.

Further professional training, in areas such as management, mediation, counselling, advocacy, technological developments or specific areas of the information world is another factor which enhances a career. The choice will, of course, relate to the individual and to the context. There is a wide range of professional, postgraduate and Master's level courses which are very appropriate to the information worker, all available in a range of settings, from further education colleges to universities. There is also a wide range of course delivery – from evening classes to full-time courses to distance and open learning and virtual learning. In addition other courses such as City and Guilds and NVQs may be appropriate for career development at the para-professional level. Again these are offered in a variety of settings in a variety of deliveries and choice has to depend on individual circumstances and location (CILIP, 2002a).

COUNSELLING SKILLS

Counselling skills, particularly those of listening, questioning and responding, are very pertinent to career development, as they enhance the individual as well as the task. The level and complexity of the course has to be matched with individual need but, if combined with personal counselling or therapy, can contribute very positively to individual awareness and sensitivity. An understanding of some counselling theories supports awareness of the ways in which unconscious needs help to determine external behaviour, and this knowledge helps lead to a more coherent pattern of achievement in the workplace. Facilitating skills are supported through an understanding of counselling, and can help underpin development. A facilitator can act as a catalyst and, through the facilitation process, enable individuals to build stronger relationships, work more effectively in teams, become more autonomous, and enhance their learning processes. Through facilitating learning, this can enable power shifts to take place, and for individuals to move into a position of increased autonomy. This in turn contributes to organizational growth.

SECONDMENTS AND PLACEMENTS

Secondments and placements, either cross-organizational or cross-institutional, are another form of career support. They provide an insight into other cultures and ideologies, as well as the acquisition of other and different skills and attributes. The format and organization of secondments and placements varies enormously in relation to contexts and cultures, and may depend on initiatives from personnel or human resources departments, or may have to be organized by the individual on a personal 'networking' basis. In addition to transferable skills, organizational and institutional politics are also transferable, in the sense that they are universal manifestations of unconscious feelings and projections. Much valuable experience can be obtained from secondments and placements, but managerial and personal issues and difficulties are not necessarily removed or solved by taking them to or working in a different environment. The processing of change is a valuable learning component.

E-LEARNING

Electronic discussion lists and e-learning groups are another form of support and information, using the technologies. Many are concerned with sharing information on the key skills required in the electronic library age and with associated training and development issues. Some are only concerned with professional needs, while others combine this with current updates on services and exchange of information. The scene is constantly being updated, new sites come and others are deleted, but all can be accessed through the Web and form a valuable resource. Materials are also being developed which provide access to key skills teaching programmes, and there is potential here for LIS workers to enhance their own skills in relation to their career plans. The uses of the technologies and statistics are two pertinent areas.

E-learning enhances such sources of information, and is a current vehicle for training and staff development within organizations. The technology is the sophisticated vehicle for programmes, groups and the exploration of ideas. These range from programmes tailored for individuals, real-time training and self-paced or asynchronous training. However, the implementation of any technologies does not necessarily correlate with an organization that is 'learning' in its underlying philosophies, processes and implementation of structures. The management of change is a risky and delicate process, and the implementation of technological developments can provide sophisticated personal defence mechanisms for managers. The concept of 'added value' to an organization in the use of e-learning requires work and attention to social and cultural issues and difficulties. Support for change must be explicit and clear.

PROFESSIONAL ACTIVITIES

Another and sometimes neglected area of career development is that of professional involvement in appropriate LIS activities and organizations. Involvement is time-consuming but rewarding. Communication between different sectors, organizations and networks enhances awareness of current issues, employer requirements, employment trends and political changes. Such awareness helps in the compilation of personal plans and an analysis of changing need. Involvement in committees, working parties and conferences is also supportive, giving access to current information and employment trends. These activities are also an indication to prospective employers of initiative, innovation and professional enthusiasm. Such professional networking is also a very effective way of facilitating individual issues and problems in the context of the wider information scene. Professional networking improves interpersonal and communication skills, facilitating skills, managing meetings and procedures, information gathering and dissemination, and also identifies areas of change. The process also facilitates navigating the complexities of large groups of people, and identifying power centres, barriers, and inclusion and exclusion devices. Networks can act as containers for frustration and anger, or for projections of anxiety, and have to be recognized as quasi-organizations, with all the dynamics of a more traditional and obvious organization. Networks can also act as competitors, and be utilized by members to achieve the recognition which has been denied elsewhere. Boundaries must be established, individual agendas recognized, while at the same time acknowledging the contribution that the network and networking makes to the parent organisation. It must, however, also be pointed out that a network can consciously, or unconsciously, act as an exclusion agency. Those professionals that the network wishes to disregard can be marginalized, excluded, or their issues not given wholehearted serious consideration. Social networks can redress this inequality, but these networks are not necessarily strong enough or have enough history to do this.

VOLUNTEERING

Voluntary work may seem a rather unexpected way of contributing to career development, but it can provide an environment which contributes to personal growth. Taking responsibility, contributing to innovation and ideas, using interpersonal and communication skills, being involved in financial management, linking to other areas of work and managing time, are all transferable skills and attributes which are invaluable to the LIS professions. These elements of voluntary work can then be used in the compilation of a CV or in the presentation of a personal case at interview.

JOB SHARING

Job sharing, part-time work or term-time-only work may be another mechanism to support career plans, and can be used to suit individual needs and preferences. Working with another person requires good time management, prioritization of tasks, flexibility and communication skills. This mode of working can then in turn be linked to further development in relation to workshops, part-time study, research, or training for an alternative career. The process has to be carefully planned to suit individual needs, and to support individual ambitions and careers. Alternatively it can be used as a mechanism to support other key personal areas, such as family, children or alternative models of living.

CAREER BREAKS

Career breaks and sabbaticals are also mechanisms which support development and, although extremely valuable in providing different experiences, may be difficult to organize if resources are limited. They do, however, enable a clear analysis to be made of what is happening to a personal career, why a break is necessary, and what purpose it fulfils. Sabbaticals tend to be limited to the academic sector, and can be invaluable for completing research, acquiring new qualifications or enhancing existing ones. Such breaks can sometimes be negotiated in conjunction with organizational restructuring, merging of services or changes in service delivery, necessitating the acquisition of new competencies and qualifications. Career breaks to support or enhance family life also have to be managed. Skills and contacts need to be maintained, and clear decisions made about personal values in relation to economic needs and family commitments. Moving back into a career will demand lateral thinking and innovation, but is increasingly feasible in the current climate of portfolio and cross-sector working.

PART-TIME WORKING

This can be considered as part of the same genre as career breaks, in that part-time working can be used as a time for reflection and change. The possibility of part-time working is of course linked to many other personal and professional factors and circumstances. Some employers will allow staff to work for a shorter period of time per week, so that other times can be used for developing personal or freelance work. This allows some degree of security while exploring new avenues. It may also be possible to work entirely on a part-time basis, but again this depends on personal circumstances: it does allow time for reflection and a possible change of direction. Other permutations include several part-time jobs (portfolio working by any other name) or part-time work linked to some kind of voluntary work, to provide additional or different experience. In all cases the financial implications have to be clearly established, and decisions linked to individual circumstances and career plans.

HOMEWORKING

As indicated, this is a growth area and one which can be beneficial to the LIS worker, and which can form part of a personal career plan. Working from home can provide key experiences in areas such as time management, developing initiatives, project management, financial management, consultancy, technological developments, networking, community involvement, and marketing and publicity techniques. The extent, technological involvement, level and content of the work based in the home will of course depend on individual circumstances, finance, expertise and ambitions. It can be full-time, part-time, permanent, temporary or combined with other work. However, this mode of working can be used to develop particular interests or research, initiate new projects, or carry out work developed by large companies on an outreach basis, or be a mixture of activities to suit individual profiles. Through working in new areas, this mode of working can support personal development, at a practical level enhance a CV, and also contribute to confidence and self-esteem.

WORKING ABROAD

One element of career growth is working overseas, either through linked institutions or services, through agencies such as the British Council, or through limited contracts with particular organizations. The benefits are enormous – experience of alternative perspectives, of differing management styles, of service delivery with a range of target users, facilitating change, training, and self-growth and development. Such work is particularly supportive if it enhances particular interests and specialisms, or can link to academic or research interests. Information can be obtained from the relevant agencies listed in Appendix I. It is crucial to check conditions of service, qualification requirements and all background details before making any final decisions.

RESEARCH

Research activities, either through professional involvement or through formal research programmes, can also enhance career development. It is possible to carry out small-scale research while also maintaining other work commitments, or to link research with a career break through taking up a research post for a limited or specifically contracted period of time. This in turn can lead to opportunities in publishing articles in the professional press, or publishing and contributing to research findings. These activities in turn support networking, and the enhancement of communication and negotiating skills. Research can also be part of advanced study at postgraduate level or Master's level, and so acts as an element in a programme of further professional and personal education as indicated above.

CHARTERSHIP

For the information professional, the key Charter scheme operated by the Chartered Institute of Library and Information Professionals is underpinned by the continuing professional programme, indicated earlier in this chapter. The new Framework of Qualifications, and the supporting training, is central to the profession. Marion Huckle (2002) outlines the scheme, and current details are available from the Institute. These are clearly set out in the booklet provided (CILIP, 2002b). This training is relevant, designed by professionals and, equally important, provides access to groups and networks of professionals with similar backgrounds and needs. Continuing professional development (CPD) is a central element in career and talent management and growth. The Institute also provides help in job searches, compilation of CVs and personal support in career development.

CAREER CHANGE – GUIDANCE

For some LIS workers there may come a stage in their careers, or even at the beginning of their careers, when it is clear that another area of work may be much more fulfilling and appropriate for them. Sometimes this may be a clear choice, gained either from experience on a placement, or from discussing other career paths with peers, but on other occasions expert advice may be needed. Any form of career guidance is 'client centred' (Institute of Career Guidance, 2001) and a career guidance practitioner will work from this basic premise. Support will be given to identify personal interests, abilities, options, and the necessary action needed to take the chosen option. This is an important support mechanism for alternative career pathways.

THE DYNAMICS AND PROCESSES

The support for any such change also has to be identified, and may take place over a long or short period of time. The process of identifying and measuring change in relation to the identified elements for each individual will also have to be managed with sensitivity and an awareness of different needs and range of support mechanisms. Strategies, tasks and measurements will have to be devised which fit the individual's personal and contextual framework or support. Reviewing, reframing and processing have to be built into the process.

To do this implies wide experience on the part of the facilitator, appropriate training, creativity and sensitivity. It also implies a professional training which adheres to a recognized code of ethics. In addition it demands an understanding of social and educational issues, of gender and race, as well as those of social exclusion or other difficulties. Individuals and those supporting them also need to be fully conversant with organizational support and dynamics.

Internal or staff development programmes, regardless of sophistication, size or content, derive from an analysis of need (corporate, group and individual), programme design (which may include using internal or external programmes, formal or informal, centralized or local, team-based or devolved), clarity of identified outcomes, implementation, clarity of strategies, and assessment and evaluation. Review and change then follows as an integral part of the cycle. Confidentiality and individual follow-up underpins such a programme. The individual person can utilize such programmes and frameworks in a way that is appropriate to the context in which he or she works.

These mechanisms do, however, have to be seen within the context of political and organizational dynamics, and issues of gender and race are again important. Strategies and models may not be applied in appropriate or supportive ways in every organization, and the existence of any such support system does not necessarily imply best practice. Rigidity and value judgements can detract from the system. The concept of 'judgement', particularly in relation to pay and promotion, can sometimes be perceived as punitive. Also, some systems are much more concerned with mechanisms which are intended to support promotion rather than supporting individual development, and this can lead to an emphasis on structure rather than on individuals. Systems can be bureaucratized so that the individual becomes less important than the system, and research on the efficiency outcomes of such schemes is relatively limited. Costings and political agendas can also detract from the process. Resources need to be available to implement findings and to support maintenance costs. The review and assessment of such systems is relatively sophisticated and can also present risks to the organization. This can mean that they may operate at a very superficial level to prevent any tensions and defend against difficulties. Systems may be in place, but not necessarily sensitive to a range of issues.

The dynamics of support programmes, driven by the planners of the product or process, interact with the dynamics of those consuming them, and will affect the ways and extent to which development takes place. Marginalized activities will create disaffection and withdrawal, while a well-centred, well-resourced and supported programme will enable change and development to take place much more effectively. Relationships and collaboration with other departments and institutions or training organizations will also affect the efficacy of any development. Innovation and dynamic ideas will grow from creative interaction.

Individuals will also have to be clear what they want from any broad management development programme, which can be any one or a combination of those indicated above. The key is to know what is wanted and needed to support individual career plans. Wider organizational objectives do not necessarily relate to individual objectives. Clarity about individual objectives prevents any resentment on being 'given' an agenda from another person, and enables the individual to analyse his or her own needs and then try to determine if these have been or are being met. Purpose and implementation of need must be clearly defined, in order to clarify the relationship of any programme to the growth of the individual.

Lack of clarity will also affect the worker who is not achieving well, and who feels victimized or persecuted by the agency as a result of deep personal insecurity. It is possible that he or she will not develop any meaningful change in attitude or work. Any feelings of need will be denied, but can be clearly observed through a range of behaviours. Alternatively, workers may dramatize need, to cover internal insecurity, or be over- or under-demanding – to cover internal doubts and uncertainties. These processes need to be understood by all those involved in career development. At the heart of all this lies a relationship – if this relationship supports need, then the results of the facilitation, advice, support or guidance will be positive. The integration of a range of emotions, ideas and intellectual input provides a platform for growth and so for career change and development.

DEVELOPMENT MODELS

There are also some frequently used models of development, which have clear parameters and which are appropriate to some circumstances and personalities. They provide a clear-cut foundation for development, with equally clear targets and goals. These models may be used on their own, or as part of an integrated programme of support for the individual or the group.

Egan's (1998) model of change and development is one that is frequently used in relation to personal and career growth. This is based on the concept of problem management and problem solving. The process involves enabling the worker to find a solution which is appropriate to his or her problems. There are three clearly defined stages to the process – exploring and defining current difficulties, defining a preferred scenario, and establishing actions and scenarios which lead to the preferred scenario. Goals and objectives are an integrated part of the process. This approach can be used as a very effective framework for development using ideas or strategies which may be particularly pertinent to a specific situation and individual. It is a very pragmatic, if Euro-centred, approach and so is useful in particular areas of careers counselling and development.

Another counselling model known as self-confirmation is also pertinent to career development. It is based on the premise that individuals act (at work or home) in ways which affirm their own self-concepts. The sense of self generates needs and ideas. This then leads to patterns of behaviour which support this sense of self, and not to behaviours which do not support the sense of self. If there is any distortion in the feedback process to self, then difficulties arise. This may have a clear impact on achievement at work, under-achievement, ambition, relationships and social interactions. Again a clearer understanding of a process such as this may help the worker to establish clearer ideas related to career and work.

Another popular model is the DOTS analysis, with four elements which enable the management of career development (Law and Watts, 1977). D relates to decisions, O to opportunities, T to the period of transition, and S to self. This is a very clear model which takes account of personal issues, but is rather isolationist in its approach, and does not always take sufficient note of complex external issues and events. It also excludes a major focus on internal feelings and thoughts, and the necessity to be part of a network or networks. There is also a need to be involved in a learning process if careers are to be changed, modified or enhanced. The learning style will vary from person to person, and so models will have to be linked to the individual construct.

Other support relationships and development processes and models include training, on- and off-the-job, as well as applying for new jobs. These give valuable feedback on the current state of the markets and so contribute to updating areas of weakness. Professional involvement is another key growth area. Reading and being abreast of the current literature is also essential. Exhibitions and conferences provide a rich source of information exchange, personal creativity and support networks. Utilizing the technologies and, of course, the Internet also supports change. That, too, has hidden agendas. There has been a move for some people from 'I saw it in the paper and so it must be true' to 'I found it on the Internet and so it must be true'. Phantasies and wishes can be easily projected into new technological formats, which will then provide the perfect answer to every issue. The technologies can also be used to detract from career growth, as they can be used as a vehicle for avoiding issues, through involvement which is excessive or neurotic. The reverse also holds true – they can be an exciting avenue to other possibilities and potentials, or to alternative careers. Technological competence is no longer a 'fringe benefit' but integral to the development of any LIS worker. The future is expanding and changing, and this provides endless career possibilities or career combinations. Web design and management, advertising, marketing, information design and presentation are just a few of the areas of rapid expansion.

DEVELOPMENT OF THE SELF

Each worker will have his or her own highly individual history of upbringing, parental relationships, family dynamics and unconscious wishes and desires which are brought to the work situation. As has been illustrated, the external world is constantly informed by the unconscious internal world. Work and career choices stem largely from these processes and relationships. Some of these influences can be clearly seen in the case studies. Brief attention to the importance of influences during growth from babyhood to adulthood can help illuminate a pattern of work and career choice and development. The theories have informed counselling, career work, training, CPD (continuous personal development) programmes, mentoring and coaching, among others.

The foundations for much thinking about childhood development were laid by Freud (1986) with a clear indication of the distinct phases through which a child passes or grows. These were identified as psychosexual phases, but at the same time Freud was clear about the key importance of parental and family relationships. Parental responses to the development of the child were the basis of much behaviour in later life. The innate quality of that relationship between parent and child was the key factor. He also identified the unconscious internal world and the conscious observable external world as separate but also vitally interconnected.

Since Freud, many other academics and psychologists have worked on the links between observable adult behaviours and childhood experiences, with some placing more emphasis on the unconscious world than others. But all in the psychodynamic tradition are agreed on the importance of early relationships and experiences. Early relationships will determine behaviours in later life and, inevitably, those which occur at work.

Other important writers include Erikson (1950), who further developed the concept of clear and observable stages in child development, with the emphasis on the relationship between child and mother. Melanie Klein (1987) worked on the relationship between mother and child in the very early months of life, and she shifted the focus of Freud's work to an earlier age. Her work was seminal, as she observed children at play, and her theories are derived from this observation, the first time that this had happened. She provided a strong foundation for much later work. The concept of object relations was manifested by her, and as a result of relationships experienced in childhood, she defined ways in which the adult then defends against emotional pain. These defence mechanisms are clearly seen in the workplace.

She identified the process of splitting, a psychic process of defending against pain. It is a developmental process whereby difficult or bad objects or processes are separated and projected into another object or person, initially the mother. This other object or person can then be seen and experienced as persecutory or difficult. But as part of infantile development, there is also a need for 'good' things and objects, such as mother, and so there is a reverse set of emotions. With emotional growth comes the recognition that good and bad are in fact part of the same person – the mother. This concept of recognizing difference and holding it is an indication of emotional maturity. At times of difficulty and perceived attack, this unconscious defence process enables the worker to see things, processes or other staff in clear terms, and enables him or her to label those that are unpleasant, unbearable or perceived as persecutory as 'bad', so that they can then be denigrated. Good things or people at work can conversely be idolized. The process derives from the parental containing, or not, of the child, to provide a strong base for emotional growth. She also identified the process of projection, through which unpleasant or difficult feelings are attributed to others, never to the self. This interpersonal process is often exhibited in the workplace.

The terms used to describe these unconscious processes, exhibited at work or home, are also those that have moved into general parlance, but which exhibit their origins. The term paranoid-schizoid is used to describe this splitting process, in which the paranoid element is the persecutory person or organization, and schizoid indicates the splitting or objects into 'good' and 'bad'. The term depressive position is used to describe the holding together of the ambivalent feelings of love and hate. Holding feelings and having them contained is a key part of emotional development and provides the foundation for more secure relationships in later life, including the work situation.

John Bowlby (1979) also worked on childhood and its psychosexual experiences. He was also particularly interested in (and explored the ways in which) attachments which are formed in very early life affect attachment and loss in later life (Bowlby, 1984). Crucial life experiences at an early age can affect attachments later. If these are not good at an early age, then it becomes much more difficult for the person to make attachments in later life. Bowlby and his work illustrated the 'causal relationship between loss of maternal care in the early years and disturbed personality development' (Bowlby, 1979, p. 45). Evidence of this can often be seen in the workplace – constant moving of jobs, no close friends or groups at work, and a fear of being close to anyone or anything. The fear of loss is greater than the fear of being alone. The strength of early relationships has to be strong enough to allow mature but independent growth. Winnicott (1965) also wrote about these issues, and the need for a 'good enough' mother to contain the child. Perfection was not necessary, but a good enough relationship was. Both these writers stressed the importance of early relationships, and attachment to a containing parental figure to provide a foundation for emotional growth.

A mature approach to the world of work is possible for those people who have had a more integrated relationship with their parents, and do not see work as a 'constant' parent, who has to provide everything without any effort on the part of the worker. The 'why don't they...' syndrome is illustrative of these deep infantilized feelings, projected into the workplace and the job. An integrated personality finds it easier to negotiate new situations and new jobs, and to relate to new situations. There is a closer relationship for such people between self and work. The more integrated personalities also find it easier to leave old situations, mourn their loss, and then work and attach themselves to new situations. An indication of difficulties in this area is typified by the 'in my last job' refrain. This indicates a strong attachment to previous places and work, and so it becomes difficult for the insecure to move on and make new attachments. Those who find loss difficult also tend to stay in jobs for many years because the prospect of moving is too frightening. The fear of loss is also manifested in the workplace by workers who tend to constantly move on to new jobs within a very short space of time and do not become integrated with any other workers or groups. Constant movement prevents the processing of any related feelings of loss or attachment.

Those workers who are also more integrated in relation to their internal and external worlds, and who are able to link the two, are bringing both these worlds together, as well as a range of experiences. Those who have experienced integration very early in life, as well as in later life, are more able to deal with work in a mature way. This indicates that the defences indicated in the paranoid-schizoid position have been worked through, and that many internal conflicts have been resolved. Work can act as a symbol of this complex process, and as a clear indication of maturity. As part of this maturity, work is an object or process which is what it is, and is not representing any earlier and major unresolved conflict. If it is used to resolve conflicts, then it becomes equated with past experiences, and is not the reality of the present. This awareness can again help in the analysis of work and career development.

REVIEWING THE PROCESS

The review of the process of development needs to be matched against the questions about self, and the actualization of ambitions and support. Such a review could be carried out in cooperation with a mentor, counsellor, action learning group, or other personal support mechanism, so that clarity and rigour are maintained. It may also take courage to realize that some ambitions have not fulfilled, and to recognize and acknowledge the reasons for this. But it may also be very positive to perceive and acknowledge growth at a very personal and individual level. This can then provide the foundation for further development.

There is also a need to consider the parameters and context of the more formal relationships which are involved in supporting career development, within or outside formal organizations. In the current climate the career support counsellor has to take on board rapidly changing factors, a wider rather than a narrow perspective, a clear understanding of good professional practice, and an understanding of individuals and their viewpoints, beliefs and perspectives. Reframing problems and dilemmas is key, as is linking internal and external factors. It is also important to have an understanding of narrative as a means of communicating personal beliefs and ideologies, and the ability to use the narrative presented by the individual for the benefit of the individual. The narrative helps to link the elements of personal experiences and constructs with the external reality of the working world.

Difficulties, defences, lack of motivation or antagonism can also be explored through narrative. This needs to be contained within a skills framework which includes listening, reflecting back and questioning. These should be linked to qualities of empathy, responsiveness, reflection, innovation and understanding on the part of the adviser, facilitator or counsellor. Such support can come from within an organization or from external sources, but any support must be informed so that a realistic discourse can take place between worker and supporter.

As part of the career counselling and development process, individual workers may erect barriers as a way of defending themselves against internal emotions which are too difficult to process. Anger also prevents the person dealing with these. Also unwanted or difficult feelings can be projected into the counsellor or adviser, as these feelings are too difficult to be managed by the worker. The adviser has to be aware of this psychological splitting process, and must be able to manage the process and understand the reasons for the antagonistic or difficult projections. The processes of resistance by the worker have to be acknowledged, including strong defences against difficulties or pain, or difficulties arising from guilt or resistance to instinctive or instinctual impulses.

Also, the counsellor, adviser or HR (human resources) professional may also be perceived as the 'expert', and so treated in an unreal way, creating an element of phantasy in the relationship. Some workers may appear sophisticated and confident during the development process, but this may be a defence against internal difficulties and weaknesses. If a worker has a damaged internal world, or has had a difficult or traumatic upbringing, then he or she may need the personal defences and resistances to be able to work effectively. To remove them or explore them in too much depth would leave the person feeling too vulnerable and unprotected.

Relationships with other formal support agencies, such as personnel, human resources or training departments will generate the same range of emotions. Some support agencies may be perceived as centres of power, and so may be related to in a negative way. They are seen as withholding all power and goodness (or money) from the worker, and so are treated with anger, envy, contempt, fear, frustration or merely indifference. These relationships will affect the individual and also the group, and thus the wider grouping or organization, as well as personal networks. Satisfaction in the relationship, a feeling that good advice has been given, or relevant training promised, or positive feedback, will conversely permeate into the organization or person and provide a feeling of well-being and growth.

Agencies or support persons may also be perceived by workers as rivalrous groups, and reacted to as rivals – one played off against the other. Personal difficulties can easily be projected into these agencies, so that they will never be able to provide any satisfactory answers. The worker unconsciously wants the 'perfect' answer and the 'perfect' solution, knowing that they are unobtainable, When the unobtainable is not delivered, then the agency or person is rubbished, as one way of getting rid of deep frustration. He or she, in return, may try to become over-controlling or over-confident, as a way of defending his or her own vulnerabilities.

To cope with such emotions, all those involved in supporting workers must be very clear about their own personal agendas and emotions. Also at a very structural external level, it is important that boundaries are established. These include an explanation of what they are and why, time limitations, the context and content of the support and its level and intensity. Any resource implications must be clarified. Workers need to understand these parameters, and can then feel that they are working within a secure and understood framework. The same issues apply to them, and particularly a willingness to begin to understand their own frameworks and agendas.

They also apply to relationships with mentors, trainers, role models or any significant 'others'. Any sense of not being contained and understood will cause all kinds of primitive phantasies to be projected into these relationships, and difficulties will be acted out by the worker into the work or home context. Development will then assume an unreal quality, both in reality and in phantasy, and so real growth will be hard to achieve. Ambitions will be thwarted and negative emotions will take precedence.

If the total process is about understanding and then constructing an individual picture and agenda, then the career counsellor, organizational and other support agencies can help manage and develop these delicate and constantly changing relationships. These flow between the complex individual construct of the internal world, the reality of work and the workplace, support, and the different ways in which the worker tries to manage these elements. Moving forward from a situation of being constrained and unconnected to one of increased fluidity within a meaningful personal framework can allow individuals to explore options, change direction, or alter the narrative from a position of strength. This reframed personal construct has to be unique. It may have to be very fluid, contained, short-term, long-term, have clearly identified external goals, and clearly identified personal growth, as appropriate. It will also produce considerable change for the individual, which will in turn have to be managed and contained.

NOTES

1   See: http://survey@success-dynamics.com
2   The Industrial Society has now become The Work Foundation: (http://www.theworkfoundation.com/)

4 Managing career change and growth

Rosemary Raddon

Someone who proclaims 'I have the truth' has lost it. For truth can be seen or glimpsed, not possessed. When I see the truth some change occurs in me. I can never be the same again. Something in my personality has altered; a previous preconception gives way to truth, but it is in the very nature of truth that each glimpse only emphasises the degree to which truth still lies outside or beyond. This means that the individual is always in relation to truth and is in a state of potentia. By potentia I mean a state of movement towards...

(N. Symington (1986) *The Analytic Experience: Lectures from the Tavistock*, London: Free Association Books, p. 17)

CHANGE – HOW AND WHERE?

Having considered some of the ways in which development can be initiated, supported and continued, this chapter begins to focus on the more external realities of managing career change and growth. These stem from a knowledge of the self and a good knowledge of the professional world and of other wider organizational and management issues, as well as the demands and expectations of employers. Career change and development has to be navigated through a complex environment.

Support can come from many sources, and the information professional's skills are invaluable in analysing some of the external resources. Matching this with self-development provides a good foundation for change and growth.

Using all the support available, the worker should then be able to begin to integrate their own internal needs and wishes with the external demands of work and career progress. The importance of this relationship is illustrated in Chapter 8 by Liz Roberts. The integration of the personal and the professional should enable the mature individual to be able, or begin to be able, to identify most of the following:

- the main elements and components of his or her personality
- the main elements and components of his or her professional profile
- the nature of the individual career agenda, and some of the relationships between this, personal preferences and personality

- why those relationships are the way they are at present
- what is the ideal holistic agenda for satisfaction
- what is the immediate primary goal, and the long-term goals
- what is the timescale for achieving these; what is available and what is appropriate in terms of support to achieve that agenda
- what is the realistic investment needed, from self and from support mechanisms, to achieve the identified personal agenda.

Once this process of individual debate has begun, the next stage can then take place – in this the individual is able to manage change and development in relation to very personal needs. The management of change and growth will be an area for which the individual then has responsibility. The management of this process is the focus of this chapter. Change and decisions will relate clearly to a fit between identified self and identified career, within the context of changing professional and employer demands. The debate will enable the individual to begin to identify needs that relate to:

- the process of change, as part of growth
- the management of self and change – this includes managing the external reality of work as well as understanding some of the underlying emotional issues
- managing the external reality of change – such as job applications, interviews and new horizons
- managing resultant choices
- moving forward as a result of change and choices
- changing, or not changing, direction in relation to personal needs and ideals.

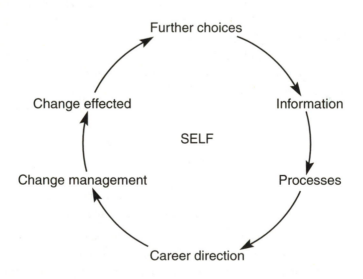

Figure 4.1   Cycle of personal change and development

This can be seen as a circular process (Figure 4.1) which is constantly being updated and revised, but maintaining core values.

All these processes are rooted in the external world of work, but the way in which they are selected, managed, processed, and linked to end decisions are affected fundamentally by the internal world of the individual. As always, the awareness of personal needs, agendas, attributes and skills, ideals and real goals in life are key elements in individual career management. The separation of reality and phantasy is important – phantasy can be fun, but trying and then failing to achieve unrealistic goals can lead to disillusion, which in turn can be projected into all areas of life. A realistic analysis of self, career, qualities and skills form an integrated portfolio, which is much wider and richer than a mere list of qualifications. Such a personal and holistic portfolio can then form the foundation of career development, career flexibility and personal awareness.

PERSONAL ATTRIBUTES AND VALUES

A personal skills and qualities inventory is the basis for growth and a good starting point for managing the change process. This can be achieved through the support mechanisms outlined in Chapter 3, as well as through personal knowledge. Some pertinent questions about the self are outlined in Chapter 2, but others also need to be addressed in the context of managing change. They include:

- What are your marketable qualities?
- What are your apparent areas of comparative weakness that detract from your portfolio?
- Can you identify your own skills portfolio?
  - what skills do you have?
  - what skills do you need?
  - what skills need developing?
  - how do you acquire new skills?
  - where and when do you want to use them?
  - are they skills that are crucial to your personality?
  - what support will enable you to develop latent skills?
  - can you accept support?
  - can you process support?
- Do you relate well and depend on other people, or do you prefer your own company?
- Do you obtain stimulus and ideas from the external environment?
- Do you obtain stimulus and ideas from your own internal world?
- Does a team or a one-person working context appeal most to you?
- Do you have radical ideas?

- Are you an innovator?
- Can you think laterally and problem solve?
- Are you motivated and do you respond well to challenges?
- Do you function best in a structured or unstructured situation?
- Do you like taking responsibility?
- Can you demonstrate sensitivity as well as strength?
- What and where do you want to be in five or ten years' time?
- Have you made any plans to remedy any gaps and spaces in that portfolio?
- Are you a people-driven person or a systems-driven person?
- Are you casual, organized, able to stand stress, driven or a driver?
- Are you enthused by the concept of lifelong learning and continuous personal development?
- What working context is most comfortable for you?
- What specific events and drivers stimulate you?
- What events and drivers cause you loss of interest?
- Can you identify some of your qualities which are positive, such as being proactive, intuitive, analytical, perceptive, creative, organized, sensitive, communicative, politically aware, motivated and sensitive to others?
- Can you identify some of your qualities which may be less positive, such as being judgemental, lacking in confidence, driven by detail, poor at communicating, needing constant support, unable to analyse situations and people, dependent, and lacking in drive and initiative?

This process of personal analysis and subsequent management of the related tasks and processes is vital to linking the individual persona to the work context and to specific jobs.

Part of this compilation of the personal portfolio should include another element, a contextual analysis of the professional scene, and what developments are occurring and also for what reasons. An understanding and interest in professional developments provides a framework for growth. This framework then provides the setting for an analysis of the current working context and job, and the dynamics of this context – identifying which areas are satisfying and interesting, and which are not, which are supporting the individual career and why, and which are not and why, and what additional experience or training is needed.

This analysis of work and career elements, both positive and negative, contributes to the overall and integrated personal analysis. A further element of this complementary but work-based process is to identify the satisfaction drivers, but focusing entirely on the work context. This should name the elements of work that are important to you, and then give each one a ranking indicating the extent to which you are feeling satisfied in your present post in relation to this element. The standard rating of 1 (to indicate a low level of satisfaction) to 5 (indicating a high level of satisfaction) is useful. So, for example, if a variety of tasks is important to you at work, and you are being given a suitably wide range, then the ranking for this criteria could be 4, or even possibly 5. If, however, you are only involved in a minimal amount of task variety, and find this frustrating, then rank this as 1. This process will then enable you to see clearly which parts of your present job are satisfactory and interesting, and which you are finding frustrating. It will also indicate which elements are currently outside your personal remit, and for what reasons. The important part of this process is that it is then possible to clearly see which elements are needed to ensure satisfaction in the next post, and to match employer expectations and needs with personal attributes and experience. This will prevent a repetition of disappointment or frustration in whatever post follows, and will also build up a current personal profile. It will provide more detailed information for further career development.

The elements of work could be divided into more detailed categories – those that relate to values or attributes, and those that relate directly to tasks, competencies and outcomes. An outline of the skills groups and sets produced by TFPL in 2003 is included as Appendix 2, and can be used in conjunction with the lists below. These indicate values, competencies and skills which can apply to the LIS professions, used as a similar checklist or framework to the one above, and then tailored to the specific needs of the individual and his or her career plans.

VALUES

Sector/context

- Public sector and its philosophies (including education)
- Corporate sector and its philosophies
- Voluntary sector and its philosophies
- Government sector and its philosophies (including national libraries)
- NGOs and their philosophies
- Culture, heritage and museums
- Research

Values and attitudes which need to be reflected and used in the workplace

- Creativity and imagination
- Independence
- Challenge
- Communication
- Flexibility
- Routine
- Responsibility
- Dependency

- Innovation and initiative
- Risk taking
- Decision making
- Security
- Analysis
- Variety
- Stability

TASKS AND COMPETENCIES – THEIR USES, APPLICATION AND INTEREST LEVELS

- Direct contact with users – defined groups
- Direct contact with users – all groups
- Support role, administration
- Resource selection
- Resource administration and organization
- Knowledge creation
- Knowledge processes
- Knowledge capture
- Knowledge transfer
- Knowledge management
- Information and communication management, including:
  - information creation
  - information architecture
  - information technology
  - information management and control
  - information processing
  - information development
  - information presentation
  - information evaluation
- Records management
- Media use
- Print use

MANAGEMENT COMPETENCIES – THEIR USES, APPLICATION AND EXPERIENCE LEVELS

- Intellectual skills and abilities
- Technical abilities
- Contextual awareness
- Sector awareness
- Organizational awareness and understanding

- Interpersonal and interactive skills
- Communication skills (including presentation skills)
- Personnel and human resource management
- Team working and development
- Leadership
- Political awareness
- Financial management and competencies
- Business development
- Project management
- Prioritizing (including time management)
- Facilitating
- Coaching
- Mentoring
- Negotiating
- Motivating
- Planning and organizing
- Vision and innovation
- Advocacy
- Delegating
- Decision making
- Reflection
- Self-evaluation and development

Another set of values could be added, which relate to work and the ways in which this needs to reflect personal values – that is in relation to self and self-image. This set could include some of the values listed below.

SELF – PERSONAL ATTRIBUTES, VALUES AND NEEDS WHICH RELATE TO THE WORKPLACE

- Status
- Money
- Time
- Intellectual stimulation
- Image
- Philosophical values
- Self-esteem
- Adventure
- Security
- Power
- Loyalty

- Variety
- Independence
- Recognition
- Pressure
- Peace
- Career (is this relevant, fun, steady progression, haphazard, planned, unplanned, cyclical, important, or unpleasant necessity?)

When priorities have been identified within these categories, they can then help to give a more complete picture of self. This enables individual aims and objectives to be achieved, through matching person and work, and enhancing a career pattern. This pattern may be ambitious or low-key, but at least will then be relevant to the individual and adopted through choice, rather than inertia or being driven by negative events. The use of a repertory grid can also support this process.

Regardless of the level of ambition, most careers will follow a framework. This begins with 'I want to be...' in the primary school, through the education process, and then onto further training and education in relation to LIS developments. Maturity, ambition, professional recognition, re-thinking in the middle years, retirement, and then management of later years are the main elements of the framework. Being aware of this process will then also help the individual be aware of the stages of the framework, particularly in the next stage of the process, which is the management of the job market at initial career level.

SEARCHING THE JOB MARKET

The analysis indicated above can provide a basis for stage one in career development – the key process of which is the identification of jobs which are appropriate, within the wide sphere of the information professions. This is an active process, involving clear thinking, rather than a drift to pastures greener and newer, driven by slightly higher salaries or improved conditions of service.

Identifying jobs is a key skill for the information professional, using all the basic search techniques which are an integral part of the initial training. The techniques remain the same, regardless of the medium or the professional area. There is a core collection of journals which advertise relevant posts, including *Update*[1] and also a range of linked publications. These include national newspapers, such as *The Guardian* and *The Times*, as well as *The Economist, Information World Review*, and the *New Scientist.*[2] Many of the publications appearing from the National Health Service also contain details of jobs as well as courses, and as this area expands rapidly in terms of technologies to support the system as well as the individual, information management and information presentation are becoming increasingly important.

In addition there is a range of recruitment agencies operating in London and in some areas of the provinces. These will have a range of vacancies in all areas of the LIS professions, and can also offer help and advice in relation to job applications and employer demands. They can also offer a range of part-time and temporary posts, and this kind of work may be an important element in career and personal plans. Headhunters also recruit for posts at senior levels, and this may be through recruitment agencies, or through independent high-level agencies.

The Internet is another source of work, and many organizations, large agencies and government departments have their own websites. These advertise vacancies, send details to individuals via e-mail if required, and enable applications to be made on-line, as well as offering advice on careers and the construction of CVs. Online job searching requires good information skills and these are key to the job market. Details can include vacancy listings, career centres, assessment tools and relevant support agencies, but all need to be carefully evaluated. As with all information sources, the information has to be assessed for its currency, accuracy, bias, and relevance to the searcher. Use e-mail to access professional networks – part of the job-seeking process in the current climate. However, it is important to remember to tailor the search to individual needs and plans, and not to be seduced by presentation or financial promises. Ecruitment job searching requires the same attention to detail as more traditional methods.

LIS information departments in universities also often have details of new jobs – these may be permanent or temporary; they may be specific to the LIS professions, or related, such as those in research departments. Again, lateral thinking is important, as work as a research assistant on a specific project, either temporarily or permanently, may lead into other areas of work, and into research or teaching as alternative career paths. The prevalence of information technology in so many areas is of great potential use and interest to the information worker.

Networking is another valuable source of information on jobs and opportunities. Attending conferences, meetings, joining committees, being involved in support groups, participating in specialist organizations and linking with colleagues informally, all provide feedback on current initiatives and action. Being aware of what is happening in the wider information world and being alert to changes not only gives valuable background information, but can lead directly to new jobs. Most are advertised formally, and 'advance' information can allow the individual to prepare, think about the organization, ask questions informally, and think long term about how jobs can relate to his or her individual career plans. Sometimes jobs evolve as organizations change and re-structure, and again sensitivity to change and opportunity can stand the information worker in good stead – transferable skills can be used to move into linked areas, or to move sideways or upwards within an organization, but without necessarily using the 'information' title. Networking can also be used by employers when searching for new staff.

As part of this employment process, lateral thinking can support career development. Many jobs now do not have neat and tidy labels, such as 'librarian', 'archivist', 'library manager' or similar titles. The titles reflect the changing LIS professions, and also the way in which other disciplines are increasingly using the information technologies for their own support and development. Law, commerce, tourism, transport and the media are all examples of disciplines where information management is a key element in the work. This means that such areas provide a range of potential posts for the information professional, and that the titles of such posts may include those such as 'information researcher', 'web manager', 'information resources manager', 'learning network manager', or others. It also means that searching for jobs and information should not be confined to the more traditional areas of work, but expand into other professional fields. Sources again may be in print or via the Internet, but personal contacts are important too – flexibility, innovation and lateral thinking are the key elements in the job search.

Using the technology as a medium can also provide information on current posts and possibilities, as well as support mechanisms. As mentioned above, major organizations, journals and newspapers have their own websites, listing vacancies and enabling applications to be made on-line. Computer-assisted guidance on careers is one area of support. Diagnostic personality assessment is also available via computer programmes, and as well as some psychometric testing. However, these must all be used in conjunction with appropriate personnel support, as they can be misleading if utilized without appropriate explanations and guidance.

JOB APPLICATIONS

There is a proliferation of books and programmes about applying for jobs, but there are some key points that apply to every profession and, once used in the information world, can be transferred to other areas of work. Job applications are about analysis, marketing and information organization and presentation – interviews and the actual work process complete the procedure.

The first element is to make sure that any job application matches personal aspirations and ideas. It has to relate to the questions above, and fit the overall personal portfolio and the more precise skills portfolio. A job application has to lead to a job that will support individual career planning. Any new job should fit into that broad picture, and then details can be checked about the financial implications, hours and conditions of work, career possibilities. The availability of support mechanisms is also important, but may have to wait for checking until the interview stage.

The initial research should include determining the scope and mission of the organization which is advertising for staff, its style of management, reputation, relationship to personal ideals, values and ambitions, and any long-term plans. Its information functions are also a key element. Once the initial research has been done, then decisions can be made on the relevance of the post and, if temporary or part-time or in a related area, how useful this could be to the individual career ambition.

Having made the decision to apply for a job, matching individual qualifications, experience and attributes to the required criteria is the next step. Information has to be obtained from the employer on the specific information and person specification for the post. This information can be obtained through writing, telephoning, e-mailing or leaving messages in whatever medium is used. This initial contact is the first contact any potential employer or contact may have with the information professional, and establishes a strong first impression. The impression will be composed of external reality – the tone of the voice, the style of the letter, the content of the communication. The impression will also relate to internal concepts and phantasies, based on experience and feelings. These will probably not be acknowledged in any way, but will nevertheless play a role in the selection process. This unknown and internal reaction is a major reason for making the initial contact in a professional manner, so that hidden agendas are not acted out in the process by either party.

The selection process itself may have to be through submitting an application form, submitting a CV (hard copy or electronic), or writing a formal letter of application. A presentation may also be required. Application forms should be clear, to the point, easy to read, and give the information which is required, no more and no less. If in doubt, copy the original form, and work out a draft application with any mistakes and errors of judgement, and then submit the final form once you are satisfied with the presentation. Be precise, and make sure that the information given matches the criteria which have been specified – this is to make sure that matching the criteria ensures shortlisting. If supporting documentary evidence is required, then this should be supplied, but if not, do not burden potential employers with more paper. Ensure that forms are sent to the correct department or person and, if appropriate, quoting the appropriate reference. If referees are required, choose them carefully to support the application, and make sure that they are willing to supply a reference, and that you have confidence in what they say. Diplomatic pitfalls should be avoided at all costs. This is all about information management – one of the professional's key skills.

Alternatively, a CV may be required, and this also requires careful presentation. A CV should reflect the professional's values, experience, qualifications, qualities, attributes and skills, but in a format which is easily absorbed by any potential employer. Again the presentation of information is important, so that salient points can be checked easily and efficiently. It is part of the marketing of the professional. Some computer programmes now include CV structures and frameworks plus advice.

A CV can be arranged in various ways, but the two prevalent styles are arrangement in chronological order of past work, or arrangement by function or experience. In either case it is vital that the CV is written in relation to the specific post for which an application is being made – it should be tailored to the post and the context. It is possible to send CVs out 'blind', but they have to be interesting and stimulating to attract attention in this context. But in any case, a CV should promote the individual and his or her skills – it can be seen as a marketing exercise, or as competent and interesting presentation.

Traditional chronological order lists previous experience, in date order, with the current post listed first, giving the main elements of past posts, and the dates involved (the 'I did this and then I did that' pattern). Although traditional and useful in obtaining a bird's-eye view of candidates, the disadvantage to this format is that it is sometimes difficult for employers to be able to isolate key skills or experience quickly. It is also difficult for the applicant to make this style of presentation very interesting or 'different'. Arrangement by function or key areas of work is an alternative. This presentation involves analysis of previous work, so that major areas are identified, and then examples of the work within that area is given under the appropriate general heading. (For example, experience would be quoted under specific headings such as financial management, staff management, indexing, and so on.) This allows similar work to be grouped under one heading, rather than being dispersed as a result of chronology. This is very much a classification procedure, with examples, and so the marketing process involves core information processes. The disadvantage of the function or key areas arrangement is that it allows for a considerable degree of 'hype'. This means that it is possible for an employer to think that applicant and criteria match, but to discover that this is not so during the course of the interview process – this is perfectly reasonable, but would prevent any further applications being considered in the future, as the candidate would be considered to be rather economical with the truth.

It is vital to be honest in the compilation and presentation of CVs, as any misinformation may emerge at a later date in some employment, and this in turn will affect references and the general reputation of the professional.

Avoid too much personal detail, such as great stress on personal hobbies, concerns and opinions. Any potential employer is also trying to analyse the CV in the same way as the compiler, and so relevance is key.

THE INTERVIEW AND SELECTION PROCESS

If successful, then the interview is the next stage of the process. This is very much a two-way process – the employer is interviewing potential employees, but at the same time the information professional is assessing the organization, the service and the post – the information and the projections are flowing in two directions. As with all other human interactions, the process takes place at two levels – the conscious and the unconscious. At the conscious and external level the employer, and anyone else involved, should be prepared and have all relevant information available. They should be able to answer questions, and facilitate the information flow.

At this level the potential employee needs to ensure the following actions are taken:

- The homework has been done – information on the organization, the context and any supporting information has been absorbed. It is also useful to try and find out the format of an interview or selection process – preparation for a one-to-one informal chat is not very relevant to a full and formal committee or board appointment procedure. The culture of interviews varies enormously in relation to the context of the post.
- The homework has also been done on a personal level – it is important to be clear about the criteria required, and where these are matched perfectly, and where there is room for development. Be clear about why and how a specific job fits into the personal career agenda.
- Think about potential questions – ones that may be asked, and ones that are needed for making personal decisions.
- Think about convincing the interviewer or panel about the job in relation to self and personal career plans.
- Check correct timing and place.
- Dress appropriately in relation to the post.
- Be aware of personal presentation and body language. Look confident.
- Respond to the style of the interview and selection procedure.
- Do not make assumptions – follow the major interviewer and respond appropriately.
- Explore issues and avoid monosyllabic answers or statements – this makes it difficult to judge the extent and level of interest of candidates, and also suggests possible poor communication skills (a vital criterion for most employers).
- Answer questions in a positive way to support your application. Interviewers need to know what you think, do and want to do.
- Ask for questions to be repeated if they are unclear or you did not hear.
- Project strengths and demonstrate an ability to learn.
- Be prepared for additional activities. These may take the form of psychometric or other testing, presentation of a subject or issue, a group discussion or talking to other members of staff. These are all part of the selection process to ensure that there is a fit between applicant and post.
- Be prepared to ask questions at the end of the interview. Make sure that these are relevant, and not trite.
- When the interview is finished, formally thank the person or people involved, using a style that is appropriate to the overall process. Make sure that you have given a correct address and telephone number, so that any follow-up process can be carried out.

Review the whole process (honestly), once the interview is complete:

- What was the most important learning element?
- What could be improved before the next interview?
- Were personal qualities demonstrated effectively?

- Was there any kind of rapport with the interviewer(s)?
- Did the process contribute to personal development, and if not, why not?

The main elements of this process apply equally to applying for senior posts within the same organization, or moving laterally into other areas of expertise. Analysis of the requirements of the post and of personal attributes have to be considered. The style and timing of any application has to fit in with the organizational culture, but the basic concepts still apply.

OTHER WAYS OF WORKING

Working independently from home or working freelance in more than one place also involves a career choice, and may be part of a career plan. This style of working is complex, and requires careful thought and a clear knowledge of self. This personal knowledge is important as working alone takes away all the known contexts, boundaries and checks and balances that provide a place and method for acting out frustration, anger, irritation, ambition, denial and a sense of persecution by whatever and whoever is perceived as 'in charge' or 'the person or thing responsible'. So a secure inner world is important to prevent any difficulties being enacted out through complex working practices.

Working independently may involve working from home on an entirely personal basis, involving the marketing of skills and products, and constant liaising with potential clients. It may also involve working at home for a central organization, or being part of a network of independent workers. It is also possible to combine independent working with other work which is organization-based, such as research or teaching. The permutations of portfolio working depend on individual plans and circumstances.

It is also very important to consider the very real external issues relating to other ways of working. There is no longer an organization with its structure and formal and informal social life to relate to. Structure has to be built up by the individual worker. The work place may have been considered a pleasure or the focus of pain, but it provides a very clear focus to the day. Finance is a major issue, and insurance, unemployment finance, pensions, accident, possible illness and long-term financial implications all have to be considered. The safety net of salary and paid sick leave is removed. Independent financial help can be invaluable in some circumstances.

EVALUATION AND FEEDBACK – PERSONAL DEVELOPMENT

In all circumstances and levels, feedback and evaluation, paving the way for further growth, is important. Interviews and the submission of CVs should provide feedback.

It is important to determine which of the employer's criteria have been met, and which were not met. Areas which then become identified as needing further work can then be used as a basis for further training and development. Evaluation of performance and feedback on inadequate attributes, experience or key skills is part of the management of change and development. However, such feedback can also be experienced as persecutory or over-critical, particularly to those who lack confidence.

Formal assessment and appraisal systems have already been briefly described in Chapter 3, but those working outside organizations also need regular feedback. This can come from clients, through a formal process, with the agreement of both parties. It can also come from the level and amount of work requested – a clear indication of client satisfaction. Dissatisfaction needs deconstructing – why and how was the work not received well? This information then has to be processed, and areas of weakness improved through appropriate courses and updating. Dealing with negative feedback may sometimes be difficult, and require support. This can come from colleagues, networks, therapists, support groups of fellow independent professionals, educational agencies or professional bodies. Within this area of working independently, evaluation and feedback is one of the most sensitive and complex. It illustrates some of the difficulties of working outside a formal framework. Choices on places and modes of working have to be made from an informed choice, and then managed within defined parameters.

MANAGING CAREER CHANGE AND GROWTH – RELATING INTERNAL AND EXTERNAL WORLDS

As an integral part of the process of identifying and changing jobs, there is a complex interplay between the internal world of the individual, and the external or real world of employers and organizations. This interplay involves the surfacing of individual emotions from both sides, and these too have to be understood and processed as far as possible. They cannot always be easily recognized or acknowledged, but some awareness of the processes, which occur in all personal interactions and in all organizations, is helpful. These hidden agendas, individual and collective, are all-pervasive, and so are part of the management of career planning. Such agendas are the result of unconscious phantasies coming to the surface of the mind, and in this context, the work situation, being re-enacted there. Many of these exhibited in the workplace are defensive, and used to protect the ego from internal threats. They are intended to take away or reduce change which threatens the stability or equilibrium of the individual, and are behaviours and actions which relate to particular memories or phantasies triggered by events in the external world. They can be considered as protection of the self.

The subject is complex, and there is a range of defence mechanisms, indicated earlier, which were identified and developed from the work of Freud by Melanie Klein, and explored fully in her work (1975). Following on from this, Isobel Menzies (1970) developed the theories still further, and used them to illustrate the dynamics of organizational relationships. These are explained further by Rossana Kendall, and are also referred to earlier in Chapter 3. Sandler (1992) also explores some of the ways in which internal conflicts can be observed in the external world. Sandler et al. (1992) also illustrate how unconscious phantasies are acted out in the present. This may be in the form of aggressive or difficult behaviour and can be identified as differing from usual behavioural patterns. It is a specific form of expression indicating particular personal or pathological structures.

These complex processes, including all forms of splitting and defence, are based on the primitive fear of annihilation, and surface at times of stress. Most of the time they are well hidden, and in many cases strongly repressed. The persecutory boss, the difficult organization, the uncomfortable evaluation process and many others are examples of the unconscious paranoia involved. In relation to career management, such difficulties may surface in job selection processes, interviews, antagonistic panels, feedback and induction processes. Everyone involved will be accessing their unconscious feelings at some point, and the more that these are understood and acknowledged, the more they will be able to be managed at some level.

Projection is an interpersonal defence, in which unacceptable internal impulses are dealt with through externalization. So attributes and feelings which are not acceptable are perceived in and attributed to others. This can be clearly seen in the 'blame' situation in the work context, or in the application process for jobs. Issues uncomfortable to the self are attributed to others, lessening the pain and discomfort.

Denial is another defence mechanism, again clearly seen in the work and career context. It involves the denial of objects or persons on which someone depends, as this is too painful to acknowledge. So a feeling of omnipotence is generated, which prevents the emotion of need being experienced, which may not be tolerated. Again this can be seen clearly in responses to rejection or criticism.

Acting out, as described earlier, can also be perceived in some career management situations. Unconscious feelings and wishes can be re-lived in current circumstances. These are denied but are repeated, and so can be identified. They may relate to unsatisfactory job applications, anger during interviews, body language that is not congruent with circumstances, and defence behaviour during feedback.

These hidden agendas are part of social and professional interactions, and can be explored in considerable depth. However, some understanding of their existence and an acknowledgement that career development involves the emotions of an individual, as well as their conscious intellect, can help that individual manage the process of change more effectively and sensitively.

The next chapters consider some of the other implications of career change and growth. They begin to explore the rapidly changing demands and expectations of employers, personal management of change, and the ways in which organizations affect careers.

NOTES

1   CILIP *Update* can be found at: http://www.cilip.org.uk/update
2   *The Guardian*: http://www.jobs.guardian.co.uk
     The Times: http://www.timesonline.co.uk/recruitment
     The Economist: http://www.economist.com
     Information World Review: http://www.iwr.co.uk/
     New Scientist: http://www.newscientistjobs.com

5 Changing contexts and roles for information workers

Angela Abell

As I mentioned earlier, the health of the UK economy will increasingly be dependent upon the skills and ingenuity of its labour force. These enterprise skills can be taught and developed. The development of enterprise skills is not about setting up and running your own business, although this might be an outcome. It is about developing skills in our people where they can seize opportunities, take risks and apply innovative and ingenious solutions to challenges within the workplace.

(M. Barron (2002) 'President's overview: linking policy and practice',
Career Guidance Today, **10** (5) September/October 2002, p. 19)

Change is not new and all change is difficult. Societies have developed and evolved from the beginning of time and individuals have adapted to those changes with varying degrees of success. The world within which the information worker lives and works has seen radical change during the last few decades, presenting many opportunities and challenges to the profession and individuals. This chapter explores some of those changes, and the implications for the careers of information workers, in the contexts of the 'information society' and the 'knowledge economy'; both umbrella terms for issues and concepts that have changed the way we work and the expectations of employers. Specific organizational changes have been explored elsewhere throughout the book, and are also illustrated in the case studies.

THE INFORMATION WORLD CONTEXT

At the beginning of the 1990s the information society was becoming a reality for many but the step-change that was needed to make a real impact on society and organizations had not happened. The changes had been subtle rather than dramatic but by the second half of the decade the changes were accelerating and the information world was radically affected.

The emerging environment was the result of numerous factors coming together. These factors were both global and local, and in the UK they included:

- globalization of trade, travel and attitudes
- the convergence of information and communications technology (ICT)
- access for an increasing number of people to higher education
- higher expectations by many people about their work and quality of life
- high demand and expectations from public sector services
- government targets for e-government
- the acceptance by suppliers and clients of many models for service and product delivery
- a geographically and socio-economically mobile society.

Looking back from the perspective of the new millennium it is clear that by the early 1990s the individual factors already had a significant impact on the roles that information workers play, and had begun to change the nature of what people expect of library and information services in all sectors. Those investing in such services appeared to feel that much more could be, and should be, delivered – but not necessarily by the people in post. 'New' professionals would have more innovative ways of delivering services, be more targeted in their approach, or be prepared to be radical. The very word 'library' became the 'L' word and was avoided by many information professionals as being too weighed down with a Victorian image. It became fashionable for information professionals to proclaim that they were 'no longer a librarian' as their work was now 'management', 'research', 'information analyst' or however they defined their post.

It is tempting to say that the library and information profession became very good at re-labelling their roles. Undoubtedly there was some re-naming in an attempt to improve the employers' or users' understanding of the role and employers certainly use role titles in order to attract the type of person they want. Paradoxically, theses 'new' roles may call for someone different from popular perception of the traditional librarian but the skills and expertise required are those core to the information and library profession. So, arguably, the trend of re-naming roles has been one of the indicators of the growing awareness of the value of information skills and expertise. Investors, users and service providers alike, have been seeking ways of expressing the value of the diverse range of roles, tasks and contribution that is covered by the term 'library and information services'. At the same time roles have genuinely begun to evolve and develop to reflect the changing context in which they operate. A closer investigation, focusing on the public sector and its changes, follows in the next two chapters.

One of the most obvious factors is the wholehearted adoption of ICT (information and communication technology) in the work place and its increasing utilization by a significant percentage of the population. ICT developments have driven supply chains to change radically and customers and suppliers to continually exchange information. The quality of the relationships in the supply chain are now more valuable than hard bargaining. E-commerce and web-enabled tools are part of everyday business processes and bring new ways of exchanging information between customers, competitors, partners and contractors. ICT has introduced the ability to affect rapid changes. Competition emerges overnight from unexpected places; customers and individuals become increasingly knowledgeable and demanding. ICT has also enabled mobile, flexible and virtual working to become a way of life. People travel, work from client sites, at home or in hotels – and still expect to work as if they were in the office. Students work across dispersed campuses or from remote locations. Individuals shop and interact with government agencies from home and do their own information searching.

This has had a fundamental impact on library and information roles, and on the perception of the information worker. For example, consider the success of the People's Network,[1] 'a project which has connected all public libraries to the Internet, as part of the Government's commitment to give everyone in the UK the opportunity to get online'. This resulted in its main protagonist, an information professional holding a senior post at Resource,[2] being named as one of IT professionals of the year by the Sunday Times in 2002. The public sector has embraced many technological changes to improve service delivery to 'non-traditional' users. This has involved considerable efforts in change and perception, as well as in staff development.

The following are examples of five roles illustrating the developments that have taken place.

ACQUISITION LIBRARIANS

Acquisition librarians have for many years purchased both print and electronic resources. But as electronic resources are rolled out across local and global organizations and academic campuses, and made available to inhabitants of cities and geographic regions, the role of acquiring and managing this resource has changed significantly. It is no longer just a matter of balancing demand against revenue (never simple) and managing the acquisition process. The product now needs tailoring to the requirement; suppliers' needs and rewards need to be balanced; use and monitoring become key. Negotiation and contract management is difficult and complex; supplier relationships and monitoring is a key role.

INFORMATION RESEARCH

This was once a jealously guarded professional skill and finding the right information, for the right reader at the right time – which was the key skill – was what we did well. Electronic on-line search services gave an even greater edge. Skilful search strategies and the delivery of smartened-up computer output demonstrated our worth. They also opened up a divide between information services with resources (money) and those without; between the user who could pay and those who could not; between those who saw a value investing in literature searching and those who did not. Then the Internet opened up electronic searching to anyone with a computer and telephone link and, despite declamations about quality, time wasted, etc., the world of on-line searching seemed poised to move out of the hands of the profession. As schools, public libraries and community services provide access for those not on-line at home, so the cohort of experienced, if not particularly expert, searchers has increased. At the same time other information-intensive professions became expert on-line searchers, with the added advantage of being able to understand and use the information they found. So what has happened to all the information researchers? Interestingly the value of research experts has grown, not diminished. Universal access has increased demand for access to quality information and high-value services. The challenge for the corporate or community information research manager now is to apply the 80/20 rule – to provide access to resources needed to handle the routine enquiries (80 per cent) and provide value-added services for the 20 per cent of enquiries needing a range of expertise. He or she must make decisions about whether and what to outsource, the mix of skills required by the research team, and how to provide services 24 hours a day, 7 days a week.

END-USER TRAINING

End-user training was a topic for discussion in academic, public and corporate libraries for at least 50 years, but as electronic delivery of information increasingly becomes the norm, end-user training can no longer be a topic for debate. It is an essential role of the service. The allocation of funds by central government to ICT training for public librarians was to support their role in developing an ICT-literate society: the imaginative application of this funding by authorities such as Tower Hamlets Idea Store has shown how 'librarians as helpers' can be presented as 'your coach and trainer'. In the academic arena the 'subject librarian' becomes the information consultant whose role is to help students and staff make full use of local and national resources – not to provide research services. In corporate bodies the aim is to make the user as self-sufficient as possible through the provision of products tailored to the task and simple to use. For e-government the information product needs to be completely intuitive – end-user training for the entire nation is hardly possible. So 'end-user training' has evolved from 'educating the user' to a mix of information product design, facilitation of simple access to resources, individual coaching and potentially, on-line, just-in-time training.

WEB MASTER

Web master is a relatively new role focusing on information delivery via the intranet or internet. While library and information professionals have always been involved in providing access to information, the Web in all its forms has brought a new dimension. It has introduced the information professional to the domain of information design, production management, legal and quality governance, and maintenance and reliability, in addition to core issues of information management. The organization and coding of information remains at the centre of this mode of information delivery, and the Web master, who once may have been the cataloguer, reference librarian or someone from a different department, is rapidly becoming part of an intricate information architecture team. It may not be called that, but in essence that is happening. Information rules and standards become essential; formats and metadata, classification and coding, systems and procedures, become all-important. One of the notable 180° changes of direction in the world of information wisdom has been the move from classification and cataloguing in the early electronic information days to free text searching, and back to the development of corporate taxonomies, metadata rules, thesauri and classification as essential tools in the information society. Neither phase is wrong – each has reacted to a context which contains many other people in addition to information professionals.

CUSTOMER FACING

This refers to the people who meet the customers – face to face, over the phone, by e-mail, over the Web. All services rely on them. The public library face for many users may be the counter and enquiry staff, but for some it may be the call centre dealing with specific types of enquiry, handling out-of-hours calls, or providing services to geographically remote sites. Issue and return functions in some public libraries are already automated, with counter staff only handling exceptions, and enquiry services are provided through an electronic route to a central team. So the public face of the service has become the staff who interact with groups or visitors needing help. Academic libraries in the UK are moving to this model and the focus of client-facing work is shifting to the faculty/subject librarian or information consultant, with directional enquiries being handled via 'frequently asked questions' and helpdesks. Twenty-four-hour study and converged, learning service approaches to ICT, teaching support and library services means that day-to-day support is provided by teams of mixed expertise facilitating the learning process rather than one-to-one provision of service. In corporate bodies, customer services are increasingly electronic and, in the case of global companies, may move round the time zones as offices close and open. Paradoxically, as personal and local customer service becomes more complex, and with social inclusiveness as a major aim, customer facing has become the most quoted critical success factor for any service.

CONTEXT: A SUMMARY

There are many more roles and drivers that could be explored, but the key message is that all roles are changing. Some are changing more quickly than others without any consistency across organizations or sector, but it has become obvious that the effective delivery of library and information services requires a mix of expertise and experience and that the key skills of the information worker, in addition to their core professional skills, are:

- the ability to work in partnership with other disciplines
- a willingness to lower professional defences
- the confidence and courage to recognize the need for and participate in organizational change
- the ability to articulate the value and impact of their own expertise
- real team playing – contributing and leading.

THE KNOWLEDGE ECONOMY: OVERVIEW

As the information society was beginning to have an impact on the way society operated and worked, the corporate sector was also rapidly embracing the philosophy of knowledge management (KM), an approach to organizational development bringing together many concepts. None of the concepts was particularly new or radical but, by bringing them together, Nonaka (1991) and Nonaka and Takeuchi (1995) made the case for a new approach to managing organizations and society based on an acknowledgement of knowledge, rather than physical resources, as the basis for successful economies and organizations. Their ideas attracted a whole tranche of academics and gurus and became one of the most influential management ideas of the twentieth century. Central to the philosophy of knowledge management is an understanding of tacit and explicit knowledge. The first, tacit, is internal and is made up of experience, education, ability – what you know – what is in your head. When a group of people interact tacit knowledge is what enables understanding. Explicit knowledge is that which is expressed, codified and recorded – what is written down, stored, explained – made explicit. Knowledge management is concerned with:

- connecting people to people – tacit to tacit knowledge
- connecting people to information – tacit to explicit knowledge
- the creation and sharing of explicit knowledge and the development of tacit knowledge
- the sharing and using of both for the benefit of the organization.

KM requires appropriate cultures, processes and infrastructures and, essentially, the ability of people to learn from experience and to share their learning with individuals, teams and the organization.

NEW ORGANIZATIONS

The environment in which we all work has become increasing networked and complex. 'Joined-up government' is one example: it requires information flows between numerous organizations and groups, and between government and members of society – a simple aim, but one that is very complex to achieve. It requires the ability to work across departmental boundaries and often in geographically dispersed teams. It often challenges an individual's perception of their professional status, the organization's management style and the way in which processes and information are controlled. Multi-disciplinary, project-focused and team-based working is a fact of life for many people, with individuals often playing a variety of roles. Collaborative working requires a supportive management style of facilitation rather than control. A manager needs to support teams, win resources, and act as coach and mentor. Individuals need to understand their own contribution and that of others, have confidence in their abilities and a willingness to learn. Changes in attitudes to employment, both from employers and employees, have given rise to the term 'employability'. Portfolio careers and shamrock organizations, as described by Charles Handy (1990) are rapidly becoming the norm. The work of Senge (1994), on the relationships between education and learning and on 'the learning organization', also contributed to these changes.

The current language of many organizations expresses many of the changes that have taken place. Let us look briefly at some of these terms.

Intellectual capital

It is not well defined but increasingly understood to mean the range of explicit and tacit knowledge held by the organization and the processes, management techniques, relationships and skills that provide the organization with competitive advantage. It may be equally applied to individuals who build up their own intellectual capital as part of their 'employability'.

Flexibility and adaptability

We have already noted that people need to adapt to networked and collaborative working, to geographical and organizational mobility and to a market place subject to continuous and radical change. Organizations must be able to embrace change. For some this will mean a new product every few months; for others new markets or new ways of working. Adaptability is the key – for organizations and individuals.

Cooperation, commitment and communities

As networked structures overtake the command and control structures of the twentieth century, the ways of working together are changing. 'Getting things done' is moving away from the Taylorist model of determining who should do what and when, defining the tasks and measuring their performance. In the current climate the focus is on determining the required output and working together to achieve the results. Working together is replacing working for the firm. The new way of working is with and through people with common interests and committed to goals. Communities of practice, interest or competence enhance project teams to enable knowledge and information to flow across boundaries.

BUSINESS PROCESSES

If KM is one of the most influential management ideas of the twentieth century then business process re-engineering was probably one of the most misunderstood. It became linked in most people's minds with downsizing and cost cutting, but its thesis was that a successful organization understands its critical success factors and concentrates on the key processes which enable them to be achieved. Despite its bad press the concept of business processes is now embedded in most organizations and provides the basis for understanding the resources needed and their management. This is gradually being applied to the business of managing knowledge and information and, in an ideal situation, the organization interweaves business and knowledge/information processes. In an even more perfect world the key business process is the knowledge process.

THE KNOWLEDGE ECONOMY: OPPORTUNITIES AND PERCEPTIONS

In 1998 the UK government signalled its commitment to building a knowledge-based economy in a White Paper *Our competitive future: building the knowledge driven economy*:[3]

> In the increasingly global economy of today, we cannot compete in the old way. Capital is mobile, technology can migrate quickly and goods can be made in low-cost countries and shipped to developed markets. British business must compete by exploiting capabilities which its competitors cannot easily match or imitate. These distinctive capabilities are not raw materials, land or access to cheap labour. They must be knowledge, skills and creativity...
>
> (DTI, 1998, p. 9)

Corporate capability – knowledge, experience and skills plus processes and infrastructure that enable their creative use – is the key to success in the twenty-first century. Capability underpins the organization's ability to meet its goals. That capability includes excellent management of information.

There are thus unprecedented opportunities for information specialists. The National Information Policy Advisory Group, set up by the Library Association in preparation for its merger with the Institute of Information Scientists to form the Chartered Institute of Library and Information Professionals (CILIP), stated in their report that:

> ... the Information Services National Training Organisation (isNTO) identified the size of the current information workforce in the UK. It estimates that there are 110,000 who work in

library and information services, archives or records management. However, if a wider definition of information specialist is used – 'Individuals in the UK workforce who practice skills and competences associated with the management and deployment of information' – then that number increases to 450,000.

(Library Association, 2002, p. 18)

They also said that:

... there is no estimation of the number of skilled information workers that will be required to deliver the goals of the knowledge economy and a learning society, although it seems safe to say that the need for such skills should increase rapidly ... Many Departments of Information and Library Studies now offer courses that do not carry LA and IIS accreditation. This perhaps is indicative of the blurring of boundaries between the various disciplines represented within the so-called 'knowledge' professions, making it more difficult to identify needs in terms only of traditional professions.

(Library Association, 2002, p. 17)

However, along with those opportunities have come challenges, competition and changes in perception. As the work becomes more knowledge-centric, and the skills and competencies that enable it to grow become crucial, so many disciplines are moving into the information specialist arena. The change in organizations and society that have given rise to the opportunities are also calling into question the role of the information professional as currently perceived.

What people know and how they, and the organizations they work for, use this knowledge is universally acknowledged as the differentiating factor for individuals and organizations. If the ability to create, find, evaluate, use and manage information and knowledge is the key to success in organizations of all kinds, it is vital that the systems and skills that enable effective information exchange are in place. Given this context, information professionals should play a major role in this knowledge-intensive society. Paradoxically, this is proving difficult in a world which has woken up to the value of information. Information use and supply is the domain of many professions and functions; information suppliers have many routes into the organization; the lines between 'internal' and 'external' information have becoming blurred to the extent of non-existence, and information flows out of organizations are an essential part of organizational processes.

Networked and dynamic organizations are supported by complex flows of information. Information runs through the processes that define the organization and enable it to meet its business objectives. And yet few organizations can point to any one person who fully understands, or has an overview of, the pattern and flow of the diverse information sustained at different levels and varying degrees of sophistication throughout the organization.

So why, if all these opportunities are available, are information specialists finding it difficult to realize their potential? Why are there problems with 'the fit' between skills available and employer requirements? Undeniably the perceptions of employers and society about the profession and the individuals within it are part of the reason. Perceptions of the informational professionals as providers of backroom and support functions are endemic in many organizations, within government and society. Too often this is reinforced by individuals within the profession who fail to effectively challenge these perceptions. The role of service provider has been the natural 'fit' for many in the profession, but organizations in all sectors do not want service provision per se. They want people who play an active part in engaging with the organization's goals and who see themselves as part of the value chain delivering products and services to the client. The challenge is to change the perception of the information professional as a service provider to that of the information professional as partner and strategic player in a dynamic and exciting market place.

EMPLOYERS AND THE INFORMATION PROFESSIONAL

It has been argued above that an employer continuously seeks to increase corporate capability. In this scenario an employer requires from any employee a good understanding of context; an appreciation of organizational drivers and goals, and how they – the employee – can contribute to achieving those goals. It is probably the most challenging but fundamental requirement. The information professional brings many technical and professional skills whose value lie in their application. Adapting expertise to help meet organizational aims is what success in the workplace is all about. This is illustrated by some of the findings of some of the research that has taken place over the last few years into what skills employers are looking for.

For example, in 1999 the British Library Research and Innovation Centre (BLRIC) commissioned a number of workforce studies. These included an important public library workforce study by the Centre for Public Library and Information in Society at the Department of Information Studies at the University of Sheffield (Usherwood et al., 2001) which explored:

- the match between employers' needs and the curriculum
- the influences that determine students' choice of library/information careers
- issues affecting recruitment, selection and retention of staff
- training and development in public libraries
- career aspirations and opportunities
- leadership and succession planning.

The findings of this research picked out training needs identified by public library authorities in the following six areas, all of which have implications for the change processes outlined in the next two chapters. They are:

- job-related skills
- customer-related skills

- service delivery
- management
- finance
- staff development.

Included in the findings of this study was the issue of the negative image of the profession. This problem of image and the employer's desire for well-educated but specifically trained staff was also identified in a study undertaken by TFPL as part of BLRIC workforce studies. In this study TFPL surveyed employers in three commercial sectors (banking, information publishers and pharmaceuticals) about the skills they require of staff in second stage professional posts. The main findings confirmed that professional/technical skills and experience were essential but only part of what was required. In the sectors studied there was an equal concern to match 'the person' to the job'. Personal attributes plus a knowledge of, and empathy with, the organization and its sector were equally important, as were the skills that were later identified as part of a leadership skills mix.

The need for leadership skills and succession planning was a significant finding of the Sheffield study and, because of its importance, subsequently became a topic of further research in higher education. The focus of this research was to identify the skills needed to develop the leaders of converged services in academic institutions.

During this period an increasing interest in skills development became apparent in many other professions. Discussions in the professional press and the development of wide-ranging training and development events made it apparent that all professions were going through an evolution in their thinking about skills requirements by their professionals. Among the most explicit is the Skills Framework for the Information Age (SFIA) developed by e-Skills UK (the former ITNTO and the industry representative body responsible for addressing the IT and telecoms skills needs of employers in the UK). SFIA is a detailed matrix of skills required by an effective IT professional, including business skills and personal attributes in addition to the range of technical skills.[4]

Between 1997 and 2002 TFPL undertook a number of research projects, summarized in the following pages, to explore and expand the understanding of what employers were looking for from the information professionals of the future – and that future is now.

Chief Knowledge Officers (CKOs)

In l997 TFPL undertook a six-month project to investigate the new 'profession' that was attracting attention in the business press – the CKOs. Their key findings from this work were that people who undertook this very senior change management role generally came from strategic or operational business roles within the organization, were senior and well respected. They were creative, ambitious and had a high tolerance for risk. Their backgrounds were diverse and no particular discipline was evident. The main criteria for their success in the role were their understanding of the organization and its business, and their ability to influence people at all levels. TFPL also concluded that information professionals were seldom, at that time, included in the senior planning teams they formed because they were not members of the peer group with which the CKO identified.

Skills for Knowledge Management (1998) project

In 1998 the Library and Information Commission (LIC) commissioned an international research project with the aim of helping the library and information profession play a fuller part in the development and growth of the knowledge economy. The objectives of the research were to:

- gain an understanding of KM and the roles, skills and competencies needed in these environments
- assess the implications for the library and information profession if its members are to play a full part in KM
- assess the routes available to people wishing to develop KM skills
- examine the need for information literacy throughout KM environments.

Key findings from this work included identification of a number of roles concerned with knowledge management. Some were full-time designation KM roles, others were part-time and others a re-alignment of responsibilities in existing roles. The skills they needed were a multi-disciplinary mix, including information skills, and key competences for people in these roles was team working and the ability to build effective teams. Other common requirements were an understanding of the organization and the sector in which it operates; flexibility and willingness to take on tasks outside their own professional area, and the ability to be opportunistic and persuasive. These roles required people who were business- rather than function- or discipline-orientated, with a breadth of experience, maturity of approach and ability to 'think outside their box'. The skills identified were presented as core professional/technical skills developed through education and training, so called survival skills, as well as KM enabling skills (see Figure 5.1).

Also identified was a growing recognition of the need to improve the information management skills of people within organizations – to improve corporate information literacy. So the ability to transfer skills was beginning to become important.

The conclusions were that the need for professional and technical LIS skills was growing rapidly in KM environments but for information specialists to be effective they needed a range of additional skills. There was, however, a more fundamental problem.

Corporate information flows are complex and organizations were increasingly recognizing that it was crucial to understand and manage their information. But the history of treating different types of information as discrete entities meant that there was no one profession or function that understood or addressed the whole. The LIS

KM enabling skills

Business process identification and analysis
Understanding the knowledge process within the business process
Understanding the value, context and dynamics of knowledge and information
Knowledge asset identification, creation, maintenance and exploitation
Knowledge mapping and flows
Change management
Leveraging ICT to create KM enablers
Understanding of support and facilitation of communities and teams
Project management
Information structuring and architecture
Document and information management and work flows
An understanding of information management principles
An understanding of publishing processes
An understanding of technological opportunities

Environmental skills and competencies (Survival skills)

Communication
Team working
Negotiation
Persuasion
Facilitation
Coaching
Mentoring
Business processes

Figure 5.1   Skills for Knowledge Management findings

profession was focused largely on the acquisition and distribution of external information. Although desktop access to information resources had expanded this focus, the LIS professional often still narrowly defined information horizons. Similarly, records management, which was gaining a higher profile in KM environments, had developed its own particular discipline: document management had evolved from ICT and workflow routes. At the same time many other functions have developed information management capability. Market research, strategic planning and competitive intelligence departments are examples of information-rich areas that often set up their own systems. Equally, customer relations, sales, technical support, research and development all use information management tools, and ICT professionals are particularly strong on key KM skills such as project management.

A range of skills contributed to the KM information picture and the KM environment can exploit the experience of people with diverse backgrounds relating to different aspects of information management. The new corporate roles were attracting a range of professions, such as the journalists and writers who were helping capture best practice. A breed of 'can do' people who relate more to opportunities than functions was evident, and they were attracted to KM roles. In contrast the LIS profession appeared to have had little impact on KM organizations. Whilst it is true that a few 'mature' KM environments were actively integrating LIS skills into their KM teams, many had still to discover that these skills exist. And it was sobering to note that many organizations saw a limited involvement for LIS professionals, despite the development of imaginative and relevant courses in LIS academic departments, because of their perception of a profession that seldom engages with 'the business'. Still more disturbing was the lack of use of the wealth of information theory which was directly relevant to KM concepts and available in the LIS literature but seldom, if ever, referenced in KM literature.

So the KM phenomenon presented the LIS profession with a unique opportunity to make an impact in organizations of all sizes and in all sectors, but to take advantage of that opportunity individual professionals need fully to understand the potential of those skills and the business objectives of the organizations that employ them. More fundamentally, the research indicated that the information profession needed to represent the range of skills that are required to manage complex corporate information. This theme was taken up in the CILIP KPAG Report *CILIP in the Knowledge Economy* (CILIP, 2003).

THE KNOWLEDGE ECONOMY: STRATEGIC INFORMATION SKILLS

During 2001 TFPL project-managed research for the European Round Table of Industrialists (ERT).[5] Following this research it was clear that new skills needed to be acquired by people and companies if they were to achieve competitive advantage in the knowledge economy. It was also clear that there needed to be a change in attitude to support and enhance changes in skills. At the same time, a report on knowledge management in the pharmaceutical industry identified excellent information management as a crucial element of developing a successful KM environment (Ward and Abell, 2001).

Given this context, it could be expected that the information services sector would play a major role in these knowledge-intensive organizations. However, in 2001, there was still little evidence of this happening and the information services National Training Organisation (isNTO) commissioned research to develop the findings of the LIC report, especially with regard to the development of knowledge management in public sector organizations. The aim of the research was to:

> ... improve the understanding of the information professions and their suppliers (including education and training providers) of the opportunities presented to the information workforce by the knowledge economy.

In commissioning this research project the isNTO was seeking to provide a basis for planning for the future development of the information services workforce. The focus of the research was not purely on the 'professionals' but on the broad range of workers, qualified or not, who might find themselves enlisted in information-related roles now or in the future. The methodology selected by the isNTO was scenario planning. Working with people from a variety of functions and representing all levels of seniority in eight major organizations, different scenarios for the future were considered and the implications for the information support were examined (Skelton and Abell, 2001).

The conclusions not only supported earlier research; they went further. All organizations could foresee that information specialists would play strategic and operational roles in 'inforstructure' and exploitation teams, and would be major players in the information flow between the organizations and the outside world. Such teams would be multi-disciplinary, and include information specialists, ICT practitioners, subject specialists and 'super-users'; be skilled at cross-boundary working; and increasingly be part of a virtual team or department, dispersed throughout the organization and its partners. The skills mix identified was a refinement of the earlier work but also included a range of business skills, some of which are transferable and some of which are organization-specific.

These reflect those identified by a complementary study also commissioned by the isNTO (2001) during the same period. The areas of expertise identified now form the basis of a web-enabled skills toolkit with the skills grouped in six sets, allowing requirements and levels to be assessed. They can be graphically displayed as a 'spidergram' (see Figure 5.2).

SO, WHAT DO EMPLOYERS WANT?

So far, a list of skills has been identified through research which will very likely be on an employer's shopping list. However, the shopping list is only part of the story. The 'skills' listed are:

- a mix of professional and technical skills developed through education, continuing professional development and experience
- broader management and organizational skills acquired in much the same way
- personal attributes.

What employers really want is an appropriate mix of the first two, plus the mix of personal attributes that makes the worker the right person for the job. It sounds subjective, and to some extent it is, but employers are becoming clear that personality and attributes play a big part in the success of an appointee. That does not mean that they want a standard profile. Different attributes are required for different roles and

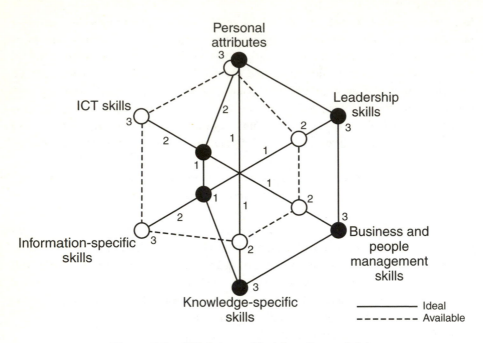

Figure 5.2 Skills balance of the information specialist

organizations, as is a different mix of professional expertise and management skills. It does mean, however, that career progression will depend as much on personal development as on professional skill. It pays to understand all these aspects, to be prepared to work on areas of weakness and to let go some areas of expertise when appropriate. If a role has a large management or strategic responsibility then the employer will look for an understanding of strategy, potential leadership qualities, the ability to influence and negotiate, and the candidate's tolerance of risk – not his or her on-line searching expertise.

Fundamentally employers want people who are prepared to engage. The professional skills are almost secondary to the willingness and ability to:

- identify with the objectives of the organization and with other people
- commit to corporate values
- learn and develop – oneself and others.

This chapter has focused on the process of matching changing employers' needs to those that can be offered by the informational professional. This has included exploring the potential of the knowledge manager in the rapidly changing but expanding world of modern organizations. The information professional also needs a framework, a process and a model for thinking about organizational life. To support the focus on changing employer needs, the next two chapters offer some ideas for thinking about and surviving in organizations.

NOTES

1   See: http://www.peoplesnetwork.gov.uk
2   See: http://www.resource.gov.uk/
3   The text of the White Paper is available at: http://www.dti.gov.uk/comp/competitive/pdfs/wh_pdf2.pdf
4   See: http://www.e-skills.com/sfia/
5   See: http://www.ert.be/

6 Developing a career in organizations: or don't take it personally!

Rossana Kendall

... The individual has to fit himself into a whole system and live for it ... however, out of this system values and enhancement must flow back to him ... the life of the individual is but a means for the ends of the whole, the life of the whole but an instrument for the purposes of the individual.

(S. Freud (1963) *Civilization and its Discontents*, London: Penguin, p. vii)

HAVE A THEORY, OR MAKE UP A STORY

Standing at the window looking out into the garden one morning, I saw something that I had never seen before and did not understand. For about fifteen seconds this threw me into confusion, creating a sense almost of panic, and an intense struggle to find my bearings. I could see that it was an object, though I had no sense of its boundaries; there seemed to be some colours – red, black, white, and beige – that I could simply not associate with the garden. With a feeling like coming to the surface after jumping in at the deep end of a swimming pool, I realised that it was a bird larger than any I had ever seen in the garden. I reached for a bird book and found that it was a greater spotted woodpecker.

The point of this story is that this experience may, perhaps, be familiar to people who work in large organizations: we see things happening, they seem unreal, we struggle to make sense of them, and we need some frame of reference to help us do that. The only difference is that we are not seeing a beautiful bird, but rather some complex dynamic being played out, often unconsciously, and sometimes threatening us.

This is a key point in career development. Things may have been fairly manageable and comprehensible so far. Then, suddenly, the framework in which we nurtured our career throws up something we do not understand at all. It is important to be conscious that this is a moment of choice about expanding our understanding of organizations. It is important for career development to make that choice an affirmative one. This chapter will offer some tools for handling organizational life, applicable to the library and information services profession. Some are more towards the practical end of the spectrum, some more towards the psychological end.

Just as a reference book identified the greater spotted woodpecker, so the first proposed tool for surviving and thriving in an organization is to have a way of thinking about it, theorizing about it: 'The psychological function of a theory is ..., in part, a way of containing our fear of being lost and overwhelmed' (French and Vince, 1999, p. 88). The ability to theorize enables us to place a small but crucial distance between ourselves and events, so that we can think and look for meaning instead of feeling bewildered, panicky or persecuted. Gareth Morgan (1986) offers a compendium of theories about organizations. This chapter, and the one on managing change, will offer some notions mostly from the psychoanalytic tradition of theory about organizations and individuals.

But it does not even have to be as complex as a theory: Mike, a senior manager, talking about how he has survived throughout a long career in big organizations, said: 'My mother was a people person and always telling stories about who did what, and I make stories about things, too.' A Head of Department, Ann, would express her frustration with senior (male) colleagues by sending ironically puzzled memos to them which retold current events as if seen with innocent eyes by Alice in Wonderland (signing off as 'naughty Alice'). Eyes, of course, that revealed possible inconsistencies in the senior men's thinking. It can even be useful, when contemplating some fantastic organizational event, to ask: 'If this were a dream, how would I interpret it?'

Whether we use a theory or make a story, we are being proactive and creative, and we are seeking to discover meaning, stepping a little outside ourselves and seeing ourselves in an arena which we can try to understand:

> ... a move which, as it were, creates a space in which the location of the feeling and its possible organisational meaning can be opened up for exploration
>
> (French and Vince, 1999, p. 148)

Mike says that 'being an observer' has helped him. James, who has moved from a career in the armed services to a specialized manufacturing industry, said: 'I divorce myself slightly from work.' Fiona, a manager with long experience in the public sector, spoke about 'distancing myself a bit, disengaging myself from work, in a way' as a means of surviving.

SPACE TO THINK, SPACE TO PLAY

The paradox of space and containment suggests a second tool, both for living in organizations and also for managing change. Areas of psychological and physical space, which nevertheless have clear boundaries, provide the secure environment in which we can play with our theories and stories, formulate, consider, discuss and refine them.

Celia, who has experienced rapid career progression, said: 'I have managed to work in a bubble.' Perhaps she meant that the bubble was a kind of protective membrane; within it she described her teams as having a participative, successful, and creative life.

D.W. Winnicott formulated a theory of transitional objects, like the teddy bear, which helps an infant to come to terms with reality. In organizational terms, 'transitional phenomena' (Winnicott, 1971, p. 46) can include people, roles, ideas or spaces. 'Naughty Alice' bought a special coffee percolator which ground coffee before brewing it and, sure enough, the aroma attracted a network of colleagues, and their information, to her room.

Winnicott also posited the idea of an area of play, situated between the infant's inner world and the reality of the outer world. Play in the transitional space, with transitional objects, helps the infant to develop a sense of itself. For the adult in an organization, we might suppose that this theory can be translated into the idea that places, situations and roles in which workers can reflect on their experience, and try out ideas without external consequences, not only help workers to survive organizational life, but also enable them to be creative '...in playing, and perhaps only in playing, the child or adult is free to be creative' (Winnicott, 1971, p. 62).

A good manager can be a containing space, as can an appraisal session, a training course, a meeting with a mentor, a staff room. In one organization, smokers were relegated to a bare room which was rarely cleaned but it became evident that the smokers formed a tightly knit group, providing each other with key information and never betraying their sources. Person, space, event – all can serve as processing mechanisms to help make sense of organizational life. It may be helpful for information workers to think that, as guardians of real or virtual spaces in which information is kept, they hold the key to a very real psychological, as well as practical, resource.

So these objects or spaces are real yet do not belong quite to the 'real' world. They exist between the real and the imagined; they are a bridge between these two worlds. For example, a training course is not our actual job, but it does help us think about the real world of work.

SELF-AWARENESS AND THE POWER OF THE PAST

James told me that organizations can be used to move the focus of personal life into work, because issues in organizations are easier to resolve. He may have been saying that when he experienced a difficult period in his personal life, he had turned his focus towards work, an arena in which he felt he could sort out issues positively. This proposition, which may ring true for a number of readers, brings us to the work of Isabel Menzies. She offers a set of theories which can help in thinking about the meaning of work and of organizations to individuals and groups. Asked to help a group of hospitals to find a new system of allocating student nurses to tasks, Menzies found herself exploring how individual nurses, and the organization as a whole, used, dealt with, and defended themselves against, the anxieties associated with their task.

The stress of the nurses' work situation revives (without their being consciously aware of it) imaginings that they had (again unconsciously) as infants. Menzies suggests that this is a dramatic world of imagination (phantasy) where the infant, unable to distinguish between what it imagines and what is real, what is inside itself and what is outside itself, thinks that it has damaged the very people it loves. The infant fears that its loving 'impulses and those of other people cannot control the aggressive impulses sufficiently to prevent utter chaos and destruction' (Menzies, 1970, pp. 6–7).

This is not, of course, to suggest that organizations are all places of chaos and destruction. However, perhaps some are in this state at times; perhaps some parts are always in this state; or else the individual worker may *feel* that this is the atmosphere that surrounds him or her. The issue for the adult worker is to sort out what element consists of revived infant imaginings, what belongs properly to the external organization, and what is the effect of their interplay. This is not easy:

> The difference between maturity and immaturity hinges not on the fact of chronological years but on a person's capacity to bear intense emotional states; on the extent to which it is possible to think about, and reflect on, psychic pain ...
>
> (Waddell, 1998, p. 176)

However, those who cannot do this often cause a lot of pain in organizations. It is worth quoting at length what Karen, a senior manager who has worked in a variety of public services, said about a colleague:

> I really do believe that some very damaged people play out some of their childhood stuff in organizations. I worked with a woman who delighted in seeing her subordinates cry; it seemed to give her a high. Yet she was urbane, well-read. So cruel. Everyone was the resented sibling who had to be destroyed, and all authority figures, father figures, were people to be pleased, with urbanity and culture. But she was a sadist.

Menzies is saying something similar to Karen: 'The nurse projects infantile phantasy situations into current work situations and experiences the objective situations as a mixture of objective reality and phantasy' (Menzies, 1970, p. 8). If we can resolve the work situation successfully, we are reassured that we can deal with the unconsciously imagined situation which has stayed with us from infancy. So long as we can remain clear that the work situation is part of objective reality, we can *contain* our anxiety through work. However, if, like Karen's colleague, we lose sense of the distinction between external reality and our inner world (forget that this person is a subordinate or a boss and begin to treat him/her like a sibling or father), then we *increase* our own anxiety and cause problems for those around us.

Therefore, the third proposed tool is a psychological one, and it is this: it is very important, in order to live a healthy organizational life, to bring these issues, which belong to us and not the organization, into our consciousness as far as possible, and to retain a sense of reality. This is the reason for the sub-title of this chapter: 'Don't take it personally.' Some of the most hurtful and career-blocking events in organizational life feel very personal. In fact, these are the very events or actions which may spring from the unconscious re-enacting by colleagues of past memories and wounds. They are not really personal at all; it is their psychological history that charges them with emotion and makes the originator and target of the events *feel* they are meaningful in the present.

'A degree of self-awareness is important in relationships with colleagues,' said Mike. Fiona described how she started to look at her relationship with one organization she was in as if it were any other relationship (that is, with a person). She saw that it was an abusive relationship, one in which her organization was abusing her; she looked at what that meant for her. She saw links with other abusive relationships in her life. And left the job.

ANXIETY AND ITS EFFECTS

So Menzies suggests that the task we perform offers us on the one hand the chance to heal old psychological wounds, wounds of which we may not even be aware, by coming to terms with current work and career realities which somehow reflect situations in infancy. But the danger, on the other hand, is that we do not succeed in handling the current work issues and, unknowingly, make the psychological situation worse for ourselves, and thus for others.

Information workers might reflect on the meaning of their work for them. Why are they drawn to information work, or the particular aspect of it in which they are involved?

Not only can we as individuals avoid anxiety instead of confronting it; whole organizations may structure themselves to do the same, in turn attracting more members who deploy defences that are familiar to them in their personal history and that also lock into the organization's defensive needs. Hirschhorn says 'people's propensities to take up family roles at work match the group's need to control task-induced anxieties' (Hirschhorn, 1988, p. 63). In other words, we choose jobs, get ourselves into situations at work, and get ourselves into organizations, which have very real meaning for us in terms of our psychological development.

Once again, information workers might reflect on whether their work situation mirrors some aspect of their family life. For example, Peter, the head of an information service, found that he had gathered round himself a management team exactly the size of the family in which he grew up. In addition, he was trying to protect the most junior member of his management team. It is left to the reader to guess who had been the youngest sibling in Peter's family of origin.

Wilfred Bion explored the anxieties of work groups, finding that work groups display 'mental functioning designed to further the task in hand' but that sometimes they function in a way that seems 'to have the characteristics of defensive reactions to psychotic anxiety' (Bion, 1961 pp. 188–9).

According to Hirschhorn, if we feel too vulnerable about the risks associated with our jobs, we scapegoat people who get it wrong (the famous 'blame' culture), and focus our attention away from the task and onto the relationships we have constructed with each other to evade anxiety, creating a 'social defense system' (Hirschhorn, 1997, p. 83). The trouble is that turning attention away from the task makes the situation more risky, not less.

The three writers cited above are all saying that there is something about the very tasks we engage in that stimulates anxiety. This may seem very dramatic, but look again at the behaviour of Karen's colleague described above. Is it that unfamiliar? Is it not that kind of behaviour that makes us feel the need to survive? However, the very feeling that we need to survive is not helpful. We need something more measured and less panicky. If we find ourselves getting caught up in others' dramas, then Karen's boundary-setting strategies for dealing with her colleague are worth noting:

> I was never nice to her. I was cool and superior. This kept her at bay; it was direct: 'Don't come playing games with me'. I kept a distance, was very polite, but set boundaries; for example, never accepting a lift. I don't have to be friends with such people, but I do have to find a way of working with them ... it's a bit like driving in a city, anticipating other people's moves and potential mistakes. You're only a good driver if you understand the chaos that others can cause.

Menzies describes how the infant protects itself from the anxiety its imaginings cause it, and then shows how the hospitals she was studying, whole organizations, actually manifested the same defences:

- avoidance of relationships
- avoidance of responsibility
- avoidance of decision making
- avoidance of change
- denial of the importance of individuals
- denial of the importance of feelings.

It is hard for individuals to contradict whole organizations which are defending themselves in this way. However, evasion of anxiety through these mechanisms is not the same as 'true mastery of anxiety by deep working through and modification' (Menzies, 1970, p. 25) and is not an effective long-term strategy for survival. Working through requires confrontation of, and reflection on, these crucial situations. And it is useful to have someone to do this with, which brings us to the fourth tool.

SOMEONE WHO CAN HELP

John, when he was an engineering apprentice, had a mentor who went out of his way to arrange things for John, and who suggested he go to university when 'I didn't even know what a university was. I didn't know anyone who'd been to university.' Many of the people who spoke to me of their career experiences had someone, early in their career, who was a role model and an inspiration. Celia explained the importance of the period early in her career when she had been 'PA and Personal Assistant' to a multi-millionaire who ran his business in a blacksmith's shop, profit sharing and sharing the good and the bad. The respect with which she spoke of him and the fact that she described her role in abbreviation and in full seemed clear indications of his importance to her.

Mentor in Homer's *Odyssey* is the archetype for this guiding function. The goddess of wisdom, Pallas Athene, takes the shape of Odysseus's neighbour, Mentor, and helps Telemachus in the absence of his father, Odysseus. Mentor takes Telemachus to one side and talks with him. Mentor asks Telemachus questions, expresses belief in him, reappears at crucial points in the narrative, and stays with him to the end of the story. I think this is a way of saying that the act of trying truly to understand someone else, to support and encourage their capability, is an act touched with a more-than-human wisdom.

So not only is having a mentor a good strategy, *being* a mentor is also a wise strategy, and feedback from a mentoring scheme running in a local authority for almost a decade confirms that both parties benefit from the mentoring partnership. The interaction supports both the learning curve and also insights into personal growth for both participants.

When beleaguered, it is difficult to think of helping others to develop. Perhaps we are even uncertain that we have something to offer. However, this is a way of building a support network, both in our immediate team and in the outlying parts of an organization, a network which continues to grow in competence. And realizing that we can offer something to another, that we are trustworthy with someone else's vulnerability, can increase our sense of personal value, confidence and competence.

IT'S HOW YOU SAY IT

This is the more psychological aspect of the fourth tool. Developmental dialogues, such as that between mentor and mentee, approach the task of thinking in a qualitatively different way from everyday exchanges at work: the mentee brings the raw, unsorted, material of experience to the dialogue and the mentor, through the process of receiving, containing and reflection, helps the mentee process this raw material into thoughts and energy. So their quality dialogue is a transforming process. Fragments of experience, sometimes nightmarish experience, or parts of the self which seem so difficult to acknowledge that we can only see them in others, all these things, owned and integrated through this dialogue, become a source of strength: 'Understanding is the first step to acceptance, and only with acceptance can there be recovery' (Rowling, 2000, p. 590).

Bion distinguishes between simply having thoughts, and being able to use thoughts through the medium of a thinking process. He links the capacity to think properly to the infant's experience of having a mother who could achieve a state of mind which is receptive to her infant's state of mind (Bion, 1962, pp. 36 and 84–5). If, on the other hand, the theory goes, the mother's thoughts drift away from the infant as she holds it, or if she reflects the infant's anxiety back to it, but with the added burden of her own, then the infant's ability to think reflectively may be impaired.

I believe that good mentoring, good line management even, can recreate the experience of having a receptive, thoughtful mother, and they are crucial to creative life in an organization. The alternative, flight into defences against anxiety, blocks the ability to think, as 'they [defences] prevent true insight into the nature of problems and realistic appreciation of their seriousness' (Menzies, 1970, p. 42). Mike told me that 'when things are tough, the thing is *not* to retreat and go into the shell'.

The themes of self-awareness and help from another are combined in a report on management development from the Institute of Employment Studies (Tamkin and Barber, 1998, pp. xii–xiii). It says that:

- really good management development is based on managers reflecting on themselves and their inner worlds
- in order to do this, managers need two things: quality feedback and support mechanisms.

Mentoring and line management are two arenas that can contribute to both the points above, when there is real dialogue between the parties involved.

Thoughts about mentoring are especially important to information workers, as it is an integral part of their profession to be guides to enquirers, and the quality of their dialogue with enquirers is key to the retrieval and production of the appropriate information.

PEOPLE WHO GATHER ROUND: NETWORKS, TEAMS AND ALLIES

Whereas a mentor is somehow in a higher position, networks, teams and allies – our fifth tool – are more like peer groups. Celia had complete belief in the capability of her teams, whom she hand-picked carefully and managed participatively, and who overshot their targets consistently. Ann said she cultivated groups and networks deliberately; her teams had development weeks, people met at each other's houses, and her room with the coffee percolator drew a network around her. John always worked with teams: 'I put a lot of time into thinking who should be part of groups' and, like Celia, had faith in their creativity: 'bounce an idea into a small group of people and it invariably comes out better'. The first survival strategy that Fiona mentioned was to build up a peer group in the organization; she also spoke of having friends outside to check things over with.

> We are 'creatures of each other' and we ignore our interdependence at our peril. To recognise it, on the other hand, can bring new rewards ... as we rediscover that our feelings and experiences have meaning in a larger ... context of mutual influences.
>
> (Roberts, 1999, p. 238)

Karen said that she finds allies, works collaboratively, gets out of isolation and that 'I have to park my ego most of the time'. This brings us to the next theme and sixth strategy. It is hardly a tool, more a state of being:

PERSONAL AUTHORITY

The dilemma of being a member of a group (or organization) is: how can I be fully individual and fully a member of the group? Do I have to give up one in order to be the other? The solution is a paradox, and it is connected with Karen's idea of putting the ego to one side: I have both to feel the strength of my own authority and also not to feel that I am more than any other member of the group:

> We must manage the boundary between our inner world and the external environment, between our individual self and the group, in order to be the author of our own actions – that is, to take our own authority.
>
> (French and Vince, 1999, p. 233)

John had clear ideas about:

- his authority and values: 'I have always tried to be true to what I believe and feel ... it's not always popular, but, if I'm true to myself, *it* survives, things come through'
- about the rights of individuals: 'I believe in the right of individuals to have a voice, to be represented – it's fundamental'
- and about the importance of team work: 'I use teams to help people move forward all at the same speed ... I like alignment of purpose, not some individual going out ahead.'

Ann said that her belief in herself helped her survive. Although Celia had never seen herself as a successful person, she said she had been headhunted because of her faith, her delight, in a government initiative:

> If you know in your heart that something can succeed, something you believe in ... I was *so* determined ... I gave them the strategy. I stormed in and said, 'This is what we need to do'.

It can be hard to maintain a sense of self in a large organization because emotions sweep over whole groups and they do things that the constituent members on their own would never do:

> Unconscious processes occur at the group level; that is, members of a specific group share an emotional experience which often obliterates individual experience, triggered off by unique unconscious processes, unlike those that characterize the mental life of the individual in isolation.
>
> (Gabriel 1999, p. 115)

Yet it is precisely in large groupings of hierarchies and bureaucracies, where many of us, especially information workers, pursue a career, that we need a sense of ourselves, our own identity. Hirschhorn (1997, pp. 1–15) attributes the post-industrial revolution to new information technologies and puts personal authority at the heart of the 'post-modern' organization

- which has to negotiate the meaning of its task with its stakeholders
- where employees' minds (not hands) are of primary importance
- because decisions (not tasks) are needed
- based on increased information.

Personal authority is about being 'psychologically present' at work, bringing our 'skills, ideas, feelings, and values' to it. It is about influencing without hierarchical power, and it is the cornerstone of communication skills. People frequently ask for training courses on both these topics. But when we say 'communications are not good around here', we take action by putting information out in newsletters and briefings. At the next stage we realize we need to listen, so we stop talking and give others a space in which to talk. Further on, we try to assimilate some of what others have said into our plans. When Hirschhorn talks about listening to others, he means being available, open to, not just others' words, but the thinking and feeling behind them: 'making oneself open and vulnerable to the ideas, thoughts, and feelings of others'. He says that we need to take risky, creative decisions and deal with our shame if we make mistakes. In other words, we need a sense of personal authority to live effectively in organizations, to communicate with others, and to take risks.

BREAKING THROUGH

This is not to suggest that we rush around being indiscriminately vulnerable. Remember Karen's point that organizational life is like driving in a big city. But it might be worth thinking about taking a reasonable risk that offers the chance of growth. Paulo Freire talks about 'limiting situations' where we feel we just cannot do anything; forces greater than us are stopping us. He suggests that we should, instead, see that we have a choice and that we *can* change the situation. In fact, he says, this is exactly the kind of situation that we need to think about changing (Freire, 1968, 1970). This is the seventh strategy, a psychological moment of decision for moving to a new way of life.

Karen said: 'I had to take decisive action to survive. I owed it to myself not to suffer. I learned I didn't have to endure.' James, whose career in the armed services was ended by the decisions of others, looked for a job, not a second career. At first, feeling that his previous environment had been much more competent than the civilian one, he committed himself to his civilian job through a 'will to win'; he spoke of a difficult period in his life, and some 'personal reassessment and learning' which brought him understanding of his new organization, and a sense of the contribution he wanted to make.

Mike spoke of his decision not to go for 'the top job', although he could have done so successfully. He felt, on his own authority, that he would not have made a good top person: 'it was a liberating decision'.

A new boss was appointed in John's organization. John, previously on the top team, was offered a job at a lower level. Within ten minutes, he told me, he had resigned or been constructively dismissed. He was asked to stay on, but only to wind down part of his functions. This could have been a limiting situation for John. However, he wound things down so successfully over the next eighteen months that he was headhunted into a job that brought him rewards far higher than any he had enjoyed before.

HARD WORK AND FOCUS

This is the eighth tool. All the people interviewed for this chapter spoke about working hard. Fiona: '... grim determination to keep going ... very long hours of work.' Ann: 'I worked like blazes, piling on the pressure.' Everyone spoke about energy and a drive towards achievement. John: 'I tried to do as well as I could in everything people asked me to do. I never turned anything down, even when it didn't take me upwards and onwards.' Celia: 'I manage my workload through energy and commitment.' James: 'I will strive to be best at everything.'

A colleague who had just earned an important promotion in a high-achieving organization, told me: 'It's not enough to work hard. Plenty of people work hard around here. What you've got to do is achieve your targets.' This is about vision and focus. It means that one has to work effectively (work 'smart').

Mike felt he was 'not focused on outcomes and performance enough'; he was too understanding of failure; his bosses challenged him about letting things drift. However, he also said he was disdainful of people who were just out for themselves, and determined that no blame should stick to them. Celia, after her words two paragraphs above, said: '... I prefer a goal ... a common goal'. John said that he likes to set goals with small teams, and 'agree how we'll get there'. So it would seem as if a sense of focus adds value to hard work.

The suggestion in this chapter is, firstly, that what blocks our *energy* is the use of rigid, unthinking defences against the anxiety aroused by our tasks. Secondly, what blocks the *focusing* of our energy is our reluctance to take the chance of thinking about strategy in dialogue with others. Instead, we flee into making action plans, project plans and strategic plans which are logical lists of actions with deadlines. This, too, is a defence.

Hirschhorn proposes 'rigorous thinking [*thinking*, not planning]' because:

> High-stakes strategic issues stimulate executives to use more formal planning methods. These methods, in turn, create more superficial discussions and less meaningful decisions.
> (Hirschhorn, 1997, pp. 123–4)

Hirschhorn is talking about organization-wide strategy, but strategic thought is also difficult in a one-to-one situation, like mentoring. This may be why some managers keep their doors ever open, rather than shutting them at times and having meaningful dialogues. Or else why we run from meeting to meeting without time to reflect in between.

Focus in groups is, perhaps, even more difficult to achieve than individual focus. Bion (1961, pp. 141–90) suggests that what he calls 'basic assumptions' can block a group's ability to work on tasks. These basic assumptions rise from anxieties; by becoming aware of them, and working through them, a group can re-focus on its task. Basic Assumption Dependency is the assumption that the group has come together so that it can depend on a leader to look after it. Basic Assumption Pairing is the assumption that the group has come together so that two of its members will, in the future, produce something that will bring hope to the members of the group. Basic Assumption Fight/Flight is the assumption that the group has met to combat or flee something.

Unless groups uncover these blocks to their task focus, they will stall. Bion says that there is no sense of time in groups in these states. That may sound familiar when we think of teams that have to meet a deadline yet talk at length off the point. Bion also says that groups acting on a Basic Assumption reject development. Given that we need to learn in teams, this, too, is a problem.

The point here is that we need to think about how to work well, not only as individuals, but also as groups. These might be working parties, team meetings, project teams, and so on.

In addition, however, we may need to use different survival strategies according to our level in a hierarchy, and this is the ninth point to think about.

DIFFERENT LEVELS NEED DIFFERENT STRATEGIES

In organizations we tend to think of the top and the bottom – them and us – or else of individuals. Barry Oshry (1999, pp. 56–69 and 125–35) thinks of three levels, 'tops', 'middles', and 'bottoms', in hierarchies. Each has different responsibilities and dangers, and Oshry offers different strategies for each.

'Tops' are leaders of the whole organization, or system. Work is complex and onerous, so they share it out. The dangers are of fights over territory and where the organization should be heading. The solutions that Oshry offers for 'tops' are about understanding each other's experience and situation and agreeing together what the way ahead will be.

'Middles' have individual, not joint, responsibility. They are torn between the top and the bottom, and the conflicting interests of stakeholders. Their dangers are of being a weak middle and of not using their full potential. The answer to this is to avoid the experience of being torn, to make sure to meet, act, and contribute together.

Meanwhile, 'bottoms' feel targeted and 'got at'. They may merge into groupthink and/or polarize into conflict with the 'tops'. Oshry proposes that they should develop a sense of their individual contribution to the organization, and use a range of strategies to deal with their situation – not just the group one.

All three need to do things that have already been discussed in this chapter:

- believe they can have power (personal authority)
- know how their organization works
- risk action that can break through.

All of this may ring some bells. Two of the managers interviewed who had been in the top team said: 'It was a question of ceasing to expect support' and 'until you understand that people work out of self-interest, it's difficult to protect yourself'. How often are the terms 'soggy' and 'sponges' used of middle managers? How often do the 'tops' suggest that the fault lies at the next tier? Of course, that may be partly projection ('it's not me, it's them!'), but the systemic weakness of the middle position invites this. How often do 'bottoms' have to express their individuality in the social side of work, rather than being invited, or finding a way, to use it to underpin the aim of the organization?

Information workers may be finding themselves amongst the 'middles' or 'bottoms', especially in the public sector, where the trend has been for this type of service to be moved down from the top management team. It is important for career development to consider strategies that take account of hierarchical levels because these are also likely to be empowering for the individual information worker.

DEVELOPMENT AND CREATIVITY

This final section is about the importance of development if we are going to thrive in organizations. This section makes the link between development, innovation and creativity. Having a sense of dynamism, growth and enjoyment of organizational life is the tenth tool.

Information is good, but does not always lead to learning. Learning is good, but does not always lead to development. Development is about more than knowing; it is about being and acting in new ways. We need to build learning from our experience into our daily work. However, according to one piece of recent research:

> Rarely do we find ... strategies formalized for experiential learning in ... organizations ... Just as individuals can learn how to learn more effectively, so too can organizations as learning collectives.

> (Bawden and Zuber-Skerritt, 2002, p. 134)

This means that each of us has to set out consciously to build our learning skills and to develop on the basis of our learning. We need to build in transitional spaces where we can do the reflective part of this: a review at the end of a team meeting, an away-day, a supervision session. We then need to act on our learning.

Fiona valued a qualification course she did on organizational behaviour, and found her desire to make sense of what was happening was of a help to her; she created 'a space to think about it'.

With Mike's words: 'You have to be serious about your profession, but not take organizational life too seriously', we can move to playing as a key part of learning. This was discussed at the beginning of the chapter. From there we can move on to creativity, which arises from play. By 'play', what is meant is lateral thinking, the use of intuition, shifting concepts and thoughts around, bouncing ideas off others (or into groups, as John suggests), being not-too-serious, holding a slight distance between self and the external reality of the organization.

Those who are able to do this also seem to have the energy to be innovative, to keep ahead of the game with new ideas. For Celia, the celebration of success with her team energized them to go on to the next project. For Karen, it was her commitment to her work that gave her creativity: 'keeping the passion gives me renewed energy and creativity.'

In some ways organizations are designed to oppress and to keep power away from their people. This chapter has suggested the following:

- if we can understand our organizations and ourselves a bit better
- if we can join up and work effectively with others
- if, by pausing and reflecting, we can develop some strategies
- if we can learn how to develop
- if we can move onto the front foot
- if we feel, with Ann: 'it's your life, it's precious!'

then we can say, with John: 'I'm not sure I've ever set out to survive in organizations. "Survive" is not a way of living.'

7 Coping with organizational change

Rossana Kendall

As we make the transition to a postindustrial society, we must erect a new symbolic framework for our institutions that can contain anxiety as the social defences once did. The individual will no longer depend on the vicissitudes of a single organization for managing anxieties but on a broader culture of work. This is the sense in which work in a postindustrial society becomes 'socialised'. It is not, as Marx thought, that property will be owned by the collective. Rather, the individual's psychodynamic relationship to work, in its most intimate details, will be mediated by a cultural process.

(L. Hirschhorn (1990) *The Workplace Within: Psychodynamics of Organizational Life*, London: MIT Press, p. 241)

CHANGE BRINGS GAIN AND LOSS

This chapter will look at some of the complex feelings associated with change. It will explore the effects of organizational change on a career, and the management of change in a career. As in Chapter 6, the main theoretical framework will be psychodynamic.

Career development for individuals, and organizational development for whole systems, both bring change. Change brings us both gain and loss. Sometimes, when the gains are obvious, it is difficult to recognize the loss. Sometimes, when the loss is obvious, it is difficult to see the opportunity being offered. In both cases, what is needed is a process of coming to terms with a new reality.

The same applies when the nature of a whole profession changes, or parts of it do, and this is the case with some of the information profession: librarians have become information workers and, in sections of the corporate world, knowledge managers; the printed word stored in buildings has become the electronic word stored in virtual reality. It is hard to believe that once there were libraries in which books were chained to the wall. Furthermore, the actual status of the profession in the public domain seems to have declined, with the head of most public library and information services dropping a level or two in the hierarchy, paradoxically at a time when there is real competition for access to, and control of, information. However, the lifelong learning agenda seems to be bringing the profession in public libraries into further contact with local communities, which is one of the primary value bases in the profession.

So change impacts on career development at a minimum of three levels:

- what is happening for the individual
- what is going on in the organization, or system to which the individual belongs or with which he or she interacts
- what is going on in the profession.

This is not to mention what is going on in the individual's private life. All of these things interact, and a career can feel like a boat being tossed on the turbulent seas of the environment. Fiona, a senior manager, said she had never had a career plan – everything had been reactive or imposed, and the only thing she had had real control over was her learning. For some this can feel exciting: John, another senior manager, said: 'I have never managed my career. I've just tried to do as well as I could in everything people asked me to do. I've ended up where I am because of other people putting me there.' He is currently managing a multi-national company.

Others experience revolutionary changes: James, as discussed in the previous chapter, started his career in the armed services and then at the age of forty, at the 'pinnacle' of his career, he was told he would have to go. He was 'no longer valuable'; this was nothing to do with him, it was simply based on age and capability. He said he had felt a little bitter and, in making the transition to a civilian role, he had looked for 'just a job, not a second career'. James went through a difficult period in the early stages of this imposed career transition, becoming stressed and depressed. However, his 'will to win' made him 'check out the opposition' (his colleagues) and has enabled him to create a second career in an environment which he feels to be very different and less caring than the armed service to which he belonged. The armed services, he said, 'know when things are going wrong [in one's private life] and find organizational ways to help ... the civilian organization doesn't always care'.

WORKING THROUGH THE ISSUES

As he spoke, it was clear that he had considered in depth the difference between the first organization he had been part of and the civilian one, had pondered the difference in cultures. For example, he said that the armed services were excellent in terms of knowledge, whereas the civilian one had 'just enough'. That sounded like a criticism of the civilian organization, but James went on to speak positively about 'not fretting after complete knowledge' and said that the civilian organization was more dynamic.

In fact, James presented both sides of the coin continually, and this is a crucial psychological process for dealing with disruptive change; it is a kind of to-ing and fro-ing between the past and the future. It is the process involved in mourning:

> Until this ambivalent testing of past and future has retrieved the thread of continuity, it is itself the only deeply meaningful activity in which the bereaved can be engaged.
>
> (Marris, 1974, p. 92)

It is this profoundly experienced sense of being torn between conserving the past and leaving the past for the future which restores meaning because it enables us to see what we can carry forward from the past. It means that the past is not written off, but has something valuable to offer now and in the time to come.

This is a useful concept to have in mind while developing a career. We may seek change, but still need to process some of the sense of loss that may go even with a basically happy and chosen change. Conversely, a career change may be imposed, or feel imposed, and that can be difficult to manage because of the sense of being devalued. At times like this we need to work through feelings which can be as strong as grief, until we find a sense of continuity, and even discover some excitement about the future. A whole group of people feeling like this in an organization can make it hard to manage change, which is why change management is so high on organizations' agendas: in order to evolve, they have to enable their staff to embrace change.

Perhaps partly for this reason there are constant attempts to re-name change, and make it sound positive, and not something we associate with pain. 'Transition', 'transformation', 'evolution', 'continuous improvement' are some of the efforts to re-conceptualize change by re-focusing on positive states or positive effects of it. There is some truth in each of them. However, what remains true as well is that there can be something very painful for some people at times of change. It is therefore important to help ourselves and others get in touch with the optimism and excitement around change. The way to do this is not to deny the pain. Rather, like driving *into* a skid, it is to acknowledge and manage the pain:

> Above all, if we deny grief, we deny the importance of the meaning each of us has struggled to make of life. Loss is painful because we are committed to the significance of our personal experience.
>
> (Marris, 1974, p. 103)

And our career is very personal.

Celebration of the past and of what has been achieved is also important. It helps us close the book on the past and move on to the future. Celia has managed teams who have far exceeded their targets, and then gone on to perform outstandingly again. She stressed the importance of grieving: 'It takes time and resources to help people through that', but also of celebration at her team away-days, celebration of what the team had achieved – 'and boy, did we celebrate!'

WHY DO WE RESIST CHANGE?

As discussed in Chapter 6, Isabel Menzies (1970) formulated the hypothesis that people use the social structures in organizations as a defence against their anxiety, and this is often unconscious. Change tends to dismantle these defences, and therefore levels of anxiety rise. When their anxiety becomes severe, adults can regress to psychological mechanisms which they used to defend themselves against psychic pain when they were infants. Klein's theories have already been developed in Chapter 3, but because of their centrality to the psychodynamic approach, it might be helpful to revisit them here.

Melanie Klein's work (1984) provides the theoretical basis for Menzies' ideas. She suggested that the earliest, most 'primitive' defence is the 'paranoid-schizoid' defence mechanism where the infant feels that it has two mothers, a very good one and a very bad one. From this comes the term 'schizoid'. It has created this very bad mother by projecting its own aggressive or painful feelings into the mother, and then feeling attacked by her. From this comes the term 'paranoid'. At the age of about six months, Klein proposes, the infant realizes that the mother is one person, that it has loved and felt very aggressive towards the same person. In fact, because the infant cannot rationalize the difference between reality and its unconscious destructive feelings towards its mother, it believes, with grief, that it has damaged its mother. This Klein calls the depressive position. If the mother can receive the infant's gestures of reparation, the latter develops confidence in its ability to make amends and to be creative. To make the point again, this goes on at an unconscious level.

The group of teaching hospitals that Menzies studied manifested the 'paranoid-schizoid' defences. One of these is splitting (schizoid), seeing things as separate and, usually, one of them as bad and the other as good. This is common in organizations, where we frequently find a manifestation of the 'them' (bad) and 'us' (good) split. Another is the flight from responsibility, and this often manifests as a blame culture and then 'it's not my fault/job'. Someone able to access more mature feelings may be able to avoid this defence: Mike, who had a long managerial career which traversed times of revolutionary change, said that he had learnt never to say: 'it's your job [not mine]' and always to ring someone up and look for a solution.

Of course, there's an exciting side to splitting – beating the competition. Leaders can also use splitting to focus a group around the fight against an enemy: or groups can choose leaders who will lead them in the fight: the team works together, is motivated, and achieves in order to overcome 'them'. However, is this good for the whole system in the long run? It is unlikely, because the mechanism behind this splitting is that of projection and disowning of aggressive feelings: Hirschhorn says of these manifestations of group life: 'this is a fundamentally social arrangement and is the genesis of evil'.

So, to return to the information worker developing a career in an organization experiencing change, these defences may be deployed by the organization and the people in it, and are likely to affect individuals, to the detriment both of the capacity for reflective thought and also of a sense of reality. It is worth quoting Menzies at length here, because her words capture what may be felt at these times:

> The [paranoid-schizoid] defences inhibit the capacity for creative, symbolic thought, for abstract thought, and for conceptualisation. They inhibit the full development of the individual's understanding, knowledge, and skills that enable reality to be handled effectively ... Thus the individual feels helpless in the face of new or strange tasks or problems ... [the social defence system] also inhibits self-knowledge and understanding and with them realistic assessment of performance.
>
> (Menzies, 1970, p. 35)

So, at the very time when we need to be most thoughtful and in touch with the outside world in order to deal with change, we may be pulled into dynamics which militate against that.

MODERN ORGANIZATIONS: THE WAY WE LIVE NOW

Change is not merely a local factor, as an individual organization develops and moves on. In fact, the whole nature of organizations is changing. Hirschhorn describes the 'post-industrial revolution' (Hirschhorn, 1997) where new information and communication technologies have transformed work and made markets less stable. Nowadays, it may be more difficult for organizations to say with certainty: 'This is our primary task, the essential thing we are here to do.' This purpose has, instead, to be worked out with a range of stakeholders. These new circumstances have changed the focus for the individual worker, who has more autonomy to make decisions, putting the emphasis on thinking capability, and requiring high-quality information to back up the decision-making process.

Instead of change initiatives having a finite life, the environment is one of continuous change: Karen, who has successfully developed a broad career portfolio, said: 'We have to accept that things are changing ... we are managing something continuously changing ... it's as if we are joining a moving conveyor belt.' This brings a sense of uncertainty, and being able to tolerate uncertainty is an important capability for modern organizational life. James was describing this when he said that civilian organizations have the ability to manage uncertainty and go ahead, with no one having a clear idea of what the answer is, and accepting that not everyone has all knowledge.

Nevertheless, the psychological contract between individual and organization does seem to have changed, and, while an organization now rarely offers a long-term (let alone a lifetime) career, the individual will not offer the same loyalty to the organization. Perhaps the loyalty is turned to the profession to which the individual belongs. As Mike said: 'You have to be serious about your profession, but not take organizational life too seriously.' An environment of instability and fear militates against cooperation: 'The loss of jobs, the destruction of career ladders, and the obsolescence of skills undermine the ability and the willingness of individuals to collaborate' (Hirschhorn, 1997, p. 6).

LOOKING AGAIN AT PERSONAL AUTHORITY

It is also more difficult to be a leader in modern organizations: '... bosses can no longer project the certainty, confidence, and power that once facilitated employees' identification with them' (Hirschhorn, 1997, p. 8). Hirschhorn believes that we have to rely on our own sense of personal authority, our internal sense that we can take the lead for ourselves. On the psychological level, this brings much more of us to our work, and it feels more risky. However, that sense of personal authority is key to career development, and to work–life balance – the positioning of our careers within the whole circle of our lives.

Successful leaders seem to have respect for the personal authority and intelligence of their followers. John recounted how, in his early career, he had shown empathy when making hard management decisions, like sacking someone, but:

> It doesn't help to be too sympathetic. It has always come back and bitten me. I've realised that no matter what you throw at people, generally they are quite capable of dealing with it. They must be told the truth. Otherwise they have learnt nothing to help them through the rest of their life.

Fiona said that she believed it is important to be honest with staff at times of change, when she cannot offer them the reassurance that they want; she has had to recognize that she needed to let go of the urge to make things right for everyone; her role was to facilitate them sorting things out for themselves. Finally, Karen said:

> You have to be clear that people aren't fools ... they get initiative fatigue. There's a whole industry out there that wants us on this merry-go-round [of change].

So how do we develop personal authority? Probably by a process of thinking and feeling our way through situations, taking responsibility, and taking action. Fiona said, for example, that she had developed a capacity to deal with new situations without support. Karen's words show real respect for her own decisions as being right for her, while also acknowledging that others might see things differently:

> There is no point in staying and suffering for me – though others have done that ... my choices won't necessarily be brilliant and wonderful, but *not* to make a choice would eat away at me.

The causal link between working through issues psychologically and taking action in the real world is complex. Do we develop our career by starting with self-analysis or starting with action? Herminia Ibarra (2002) says that the strategy of beginning career development by introspection, analysing ourselves and taking stock, possibly with psychometric questionnaires, career reviews and skills audits, counselling and mentoring (a process referred to in Chapter 2) may not be helpful in moving a career on: 'Worse, starting out by trying to identify one's true self often causes paralysis.' Talking about real career change, rather than development of the same career, she advocates action: 'Doing comes first, knowing second', but of the evolutionary, rather than revolutionary, kind. Career change, Ibarra writes, is about redefining our working identity by a process of testing in real time and learning from that. It involves three linked strategies:

- experimenting with new roles and jobs 'on a small scale'
- developing networks that have links with new work areas
- reframing our career story around events or insights that help us change.

This is a helpful call to action because it both deals with the block between thinking and acting and also does so in a way that creates a bridge for us from the past to the future.

Mentors are still important, Ibarra suggests, but ones who can help us move on with a sense of our own authority, not ones on whom we feel dependent. Similarly, Chris Nichols advocates the use of a psychometric questionnaires (his example is of the Myers-Briggs Type Indicator) and coaches: 'I would encourage any senior manager ... to invest in developing and continually re-exploring their awareness of themselves. Invest in a skilled feedback-giver or coach' (Nichols, 2002/2003). Nevertheless, it is interesting that his article describes a process *firstly* of his having a life-changing experience where he turned down an apparently desirable job by trusting his own intuition, and *secondly* of understanding later on what it had all been about by means of psychometric questionnaires and introspection. This is the doing-and-then-knowing sequence Ibarra describes.

Feedback is important in developing a career, but we need to distinguish between projections and objective feedback. A projection is when one person or group denies an aspect of themselves and imagines, instead, that some other person or group displays this quality. On an individual level we can be aware that we might be projecting when we take a particular dislike to someone; it is always worth asking if they are not, in fact, displaying some part of ourselves that we dislike. Of course, the situation becomes more complex when the other has a hook for us to hang our projections onto: that is, it is easier to project part of ourselves onto someone who already has a little bit of that quality. It also makes it difficult for the other to disentangle our projection from who they really are.

Managers are in a role that will receive many projections which are not true to their identity. How often are managers thought by those they manage to be omnipotent and omniscient, when managers themselves feel powerless and in the dark. Ann said:

> On one and the same day I was angrily accused of being an indecisive pussyfoot ['Call yourself a leader! Pah!'] and of being a dictator who enjoyed trampling on everyone with hobnail boots.

Distinct from this is measured and objective feedback, where we are seen through a reasonably clear pair of spectacles, which helps us test ourselves and our actions against reality. This is valuable for career development. So is the ability to differentiate between feedback and projection.

WHAT DO OUR CAREERS MEAN TO US?

My father, the ninth and last child of an old mother, was seriously ill for the first ten years of his life. He once told me that the clearest memory of his childhood was of sitting in a wheelchair inside the house on Guy Fawkes Night, watching all the fireworks outside and feeling very lonely, cut off from the enjoyment and the other children out there. Later, he got a degree in mechanical engineering and immediately joined an artillery company at the beginning of the Second World War, where he rewrote their manual, which changed their firing methodology. Once, he spoke about a war-time advance across a North African desert in the night, describing the battle scene as having a strange beauty, 'a bit like fireworks'. Certainly, he did not make the connection, but there could be a link between that lonely child and the career he chose, where *he* made the 'fireworks' and, as an engineer, created things that worked.

Our career is one of the main opportunities we have for creating a meaning for our lives, and of contributing to society. It could be possible that money is cited as the reason for working – usually in a bitter or cynical tone – by people who have not found that 'meaning-full' opportunity at work, but cannot quite articulate what they would have liked to find. Menzies approaches the issue of what our work means to us at a deeper level, and sees our career choices as being linked to our psychological make-up. The infant's world of unconscious phantasies or imaginings is described earlier in 'Why do we resist change?' Menzies' idea is that, as adult workers, we unconsciously invest what we are doing and experiencing at work *now* with the unconscious imaginings we had as infants. She sees this as helpful because, if we can manage the situation in real time *now*, that reassures us that we can handle the anxiety associated with our phantasies as an infant.

However, the danger is that we stop perceiving the current situation as a symbol of the past. Instead, it becomes equated with the past, we act out the past as if it were the current reality. This increases anxiety. Karen's colleague, described in Chapter 6, who treated her boss like a father who had to be impressed and subordinates like siblings who had to be humiliated, sounds like someone who was equating her infant experience with her present work situation. The motivation for this type of behaviour is unconscious and, while it remains unconscious, is difficult to manage. One way of accessing these blocks to our development is to look for repeating patterns in our behaviour, especially dysfunctional ones.

Following on from this, it might be possible to hypothesize that particular types of professions offer us the chance of finding environments appropriate to the kind of symbolic psychological work that we need to do. For example, a head of a library and information service agreed that library staff are one of the most militant groups, and thought this was because of their particular personality: they derive satisfaction from working on the front line, in relationship with the public, and the aggressive feelings that they therefore deny having in relationship to the public, are then projected into their organizations. Similarly, a teacher of counselling said she thought that counsellors were often quite aggressive people, and that they became counsellors in order to make up for this, to do reparative work.

However, it can be difficult or inappropriate to generalize, and the most useful course is for each of us to explore what our own choices mean to us, and to see if we notice any possible links between the kinds of satisfactions our work gives us and issues that might have been important for us in the past. The point is that, if we are doing work that helps us manage our anxiety, change to that work is going to mean that we need to find new ways of managing our anxiety. It may be natural for us to resist, but it is helpful if we can engage with the transitional process.

MAKING THE TRANSITION

Mike described himself as mourning the loss of one of his managers. If we have not felt able to make any choices about the change, the transitional process might follow the mourning cycle: this often begins with alarm or shock which feels like fear, denial that anything has changed, then a strange sense of euphoria, followed by a searching for the past or what has been lost, trying to lessen the pain. The task during this first period of loss is to accept the reality of the loss. The next phase is engagement with feelings of anger (blaming someone else), guilt (blaming myself), and depression. The task during this phase is to experience the pain caused by the grief. Gradual emergence follows:

> External objects may change rapidly but it will be many weeks before corresponding changes have taken place in the plans and assumptions which are their internal equivalents ...
>
> (Parkes, 1986, p. 115)

Then the sense of gaining a new identity sets in. We have adjusted to an environment where the lost thing is missing, have accepted the situation and are ready to move on. Of course this is not a simple and orderly process. It is iterative and messy. It takes time and is very tiring.

In organizations, the sponsors of change, the innovators, are often at the point of emerging and going on, while the targets of the change, the workers on the front line, are feeling anger and depression. This dissonance needs to be managed. Innovators need to stay involved with the workers.

If, on the other hand, we have felt that we have had choices about the change, or that it is developmental for us, then the process might be less dramatic or traumatic. A transitional area of experience can help, somewhere linked to reality, but not quite of reality. Amado and Ambrose call this the 'neutral space' which is 'beyond everyday organisational life, in which discovery or exploration leading to creation of the future can take place' (Amado and Ambrose, 2001, p. 96). Transitional processes, like reviewing and reflecting on our experience may help. Sometimes the organizations in which we work take a transitional approach to managing change with '... the design and provision of conditions that enable the transition process to take place at both the psychological and social levels and facilitate its process' (Amado and Ambrose, 2001, p. 15). A variety of meeting rooms, like staff rooms, as well as events, like briefings with their tea breaks, can provide neutral space in organizations.

To return to a theme explored in Chapter 6, each of us needs to provide our own transitional, or neutral, space and processes. Fiona's strategy for surviving at times of difficulty in her career was to create space to think about it. James spoke of creating personal space during his transition between the armed services and civilian life, and spending time at the gym. Ann's office, with its coffee pot that would both grind and brew, and which she plugged in at the end of each working day, was, no doubt, a transitional space for her, as well as her colleagues. In order to develop a career, we also need to think innovatively. Like Fiona, we need to create space for thinking. This space-in-the-mind allows us to explore curiously and discover new possibilities:

> Potential space is that space, in the minds of those who play, within which they still feel able to exercise freedom to explore in thought and act ... in which new meanings and action possibilities can be stumbled upon ... quantum leaps ... made.
>
> (Amado and Ambrose, 2001, p. 21)

Amado and Ambrose, whose work applies and develops the ideas of D.W. Winnicott and Harold Bridger, distinguish between three types of change. Regressive change makes an organization more dependent and reduces responsibility, risk taking and creativity. Transitive change simply moves an organization from one state to another; it may be open, where the goal and the means of getting there are clearly described to everyone involved; or it may be manipulative, where nothing is explained (in the fear that this would arouse resistance). Transitional change is based on development and learning; it takes account of unconscious processes, it provides a context in which anxiety can be expressed, and it allows for the final outcome to be shaped by the process. It is syntonic with Ibarra's ideas about crafting one's working identity by testing things out, learning, testing again, and so on.

MANAGERS AND CHANGE

Managing others at times of change is one of the biggest challenges that faces those who make the transition from their primary career choice (information worker, say) to being a manager. This means managing people who are concerned about their competence, jobs, careers, and handling a mix of anxiety, uncertainty, excitement and jostling for places. It is the resistance which can arise that most concerns leadership, because that can block innovations that the leadership wants to introduce.

Ann: 'With staff, not consulting, not informing, is fatal. I have a communications crusade at times of change ... a communications policy.' In fact communication is one of the key aspects of change management. John also stressed communications: 'Most people resist because they don't know ... telling them why we are doing things helps us get through that.' He also had a story from his youth when, while an apprentice, at the age of fifteen, he had a Saturday job as a butcher's boy. He arrived one Saturday to be told that the butcher's son now had his job and he would not be needed any more. He said he had had no idea that this was going to happen: 'It was such a shock.' He also said that this experience has affected how he manages change; he never allows news to be given at the last moment; communication, verbal and written, occurs regularly in his organizations, and he ensures that people are told the truth.

Fiona's comments about communication give an alternative view of the topic: her opinion was that the demand for communication was not really a demand for communication: 'It's a demand for reassurance – that it's going to be all right.' But, she said, it is not always going to be all right: 'Honesty is all that's available. Saying what the situation is.' People work well when they feel safe, they want security. At times of change they do not feel safe, and they may not be safe. Managers can help them accept this, they can act as a container for their staff if they are themselves contained and can handle their own anxieties.

Of course, communication is also about listening. Mike, who managed a department while his own manager was disaggregating the department, spent a lot of time listening to staff: 'You'd get everybody's history, the folklore, the spoken culture.' This validation of the organization's history (and listening attentively, as Mike did, is an effective form of validation) is crucial for helping people to close the past and move on. Fiona also made this point: 'When organizations are going through change they tend to rubbish history, but it's important to value the past.'

The managers interviewed for this chapter stressed the need to listen to what people feel they can contribute. Celia: 'Let's not impose what people have to do. Let's ask them what they can do.' Karen: 'Find out what people do well ... what makes them tick, their motivation ... what's been successful for them, and move on from there.' At times of change, staff may lose a sense of their competence, feel that their past skills are not valued, and Ann stressed the need to affirm the fact that staff *are* valued; she would often say to them something like: 'What you're doing is wonderful; can't you just go on doing it, but perhaps also add this, or do this a bit differently ...?' This sense of things being 'absolutely wonderful' (Ann) and of 'optimism' (Celia) is helpful in managing others and one's own career.

Putting up with the mess, tolerating ambiguity and uncertainty, and remaining engaged with difficult issues which cannot easily be resolved, are what Amado and Ambrose call 'problem toleration' and are a key management capability for transition: 'One's life tends to be littered with insoluble problems of one kind or another' (Lively, 1974, p. 20). At least managers need to be able to be '"bothered" ... until such time as real solutions can be found and be effectively implemented' (Amado and Ambrose, 2001, p. 20).

IN SHORT ...

This chapter has looked at some of the ways in which we can steer our careers through the seas of change, and use the journey to develop and discover new futures. It has emphasized the need to engage with change as an on-going process, to work through difficult issues with an eye to the psychology of what is happening, and also to engage one's curiosity and ability to play. Self-development and career development reinforce each other.

As a counterpoint to these broad issues, here is a final quote from John which focuses on success in the here-and-now of daily work:

> I have a fundamental belief: I believe that everybody doing a particular job knows fundamentally what they should be doing and it's the successful people who *do* that. Unsuccessful people never quite get round to it.

8 Upwards, onwards or outwards?

Liz Roberts

How strange that all
The errors, pains, and early miseries,
Regrets, vexations, lassitudes interfused
Within my mind, should e'er have borne a part,
And that a needful part, in making up
The calm existence that is mine when I
Am worthy of myself.
(William Wordsworth (1850), 'The Prelude', 11.ii.401-5, Harmondsworth, Penguin, 1971)

CAREER MOVE ISSUES

Career paths these days are complex and provide a wider range of choices than previously. Success and failure are measured in new ways and the expectations of employees and organizations are more diverse. In this environment individuals are making career choices that do not necessarily assume that continually striving to achieve the highest possible managerial level is the only option and in some sectors there is a shortage of candidates for senior management posts. In the public library sector, for example, the number of applicants for Service Head posts is declining and research indicates that there is a lack of leaders and no clear way in which a new generation of leaders might be developed (Usherwood et al., 2001). This has obvious implications for organizations, professions and customers and also for individuals who are at the point of making choices about whether to apply for posts at senior management level.

This chapter attempts to explore some of the factors which someone might take into account in making such a choice, the reality of management today at a senior level, how an individual might prepare themselves for such a transition and what might lead to a decision to take a different career path. Some of the key issues that it might be helpful for managers to reflect on when considering their next career move are:

- what they want from life and work and what particular jobs or life states could offer them in terms of achieving their personal goals
- the importance of reflecting on personal strengths and development needs and being realistic about the fit between these attributes and the requirements of a potential new role
- the importance of developing and maintaining their confidence, self-esteem and sense of self-worth
- the nature of the psychological contract between a potential employing organization and its managers and the likelihood of negotiating a contract that would meet their own needs
- the aim of developing a portfolio of skills which ensures they can add value to a role both now and in the future and what a particular job might contribute to that portfolio and to their personal development
- the potential for challenging posts to provide opportunities to develop core management skills such as financial and human resource management.

These issues are considered below. The analysis in this chapter has been drawn from an examination of relevant literature and interviews with past, present and potential future senior managers.

THE PSYCHOLOGICAL CONTRACT

The current generation of senior managers have lived through a major transition in the relationship between organizations and their employees. The pressures and changes which have brought this about have produced a very different career environment for the coming generation and managers are responding by making different career choices from those who came before them. These choices are being driven both by the impetus to leave negative situations, such as excessive pressure or poor job satisfaction, and the desire to move towards more positive career or life positions, and are a product of the social, financial and psychological needs of the individual.

The objective evidence of how an individual's working life develops is their progression from job to job, or from job to other life states such as carer, student or traveller. The subjective evidence of what that working life may mean to the individual is its contrast with their initial plans, aspirations and ambitions. However successful the objective career may appear to other people, the true measure of how satisfactory that career might be is how closely it has met the individual's aspirations and their psychological and emotional needs.

For many managers, progression up the career ladder to senior management, director or even chief executive posts has not only been important as an objective measure of their achievement but also significant in developing and sustaining their personal confidence, sense of self-worth and place in the world. The way these needs are met at work is part of the psychological contract between the manager and the organization. Many of these dynamics have been explored in Chapter 6.

The psychological contract is 'the stated and implied set of expectations, obligations, and understandings, operating between workers and employer'.[1] It is not a formal document but exists in the perceptions of employees and their employing organizations of their mutual rights and responsibilities. A career is a succession of psychological contracts which are negotiated between an employee and each new organization and also with the same organization, as their role changes over time.

One of the key drivers influencing the decisions of individual managers about their future/career life paths is their level of satisfaction with their current psychological contract and their perception of how that contract might develop in the future.

The views of past and present senior managers demonstrate that there have been substantial changes in the nature of their relationship with their employing organization over time. The key aspects of these changes include the loss of autonomy, the growth of centralized planning and performance management, a more ruthless approach to finance and human resource management and the loss of the recognition and appreciation of individual achievement and commitment.

These changes reflect the trend to move from 'relational' contracts to 'transactional' contracts. Herriot and Pemberton (1995, p. 17) suggests that in relational contracts employees offer loyalty, conformity, commitment and trust while the organization offers security, promotion prospects, training and care when in trouble. In these contractual relationships, managers assume that a job could be for life, that their employer will look after them in times of personal or organizational difficulty and that in return they will respond to whatever demands the organization may make.

These largely open-ended contracts are disappearing due to trends in the business environment such as globalization, the pace of change, financial pressures, competition and changes in organizational values, and they are being replaced by much more prescriptive 'transactional' contracts. In 'transactional' contracts, trust and mutual commitment are replaced by a more overt and specific contract where each party holds the other to the term of the contract, the outcomes required from each party are more explicit and changes are directly negotiated or imposed.

For many current managers the withdrawal of the relational contract has been unilateral and has caused substantial distress. This is possibly, however, a particular issue for the generation of managers who have lived through this transition. It may be less significant for managers who are now moving into senior posts in the full understanding of the terms of the contract they are taking on.

The nature of these contracts and the balance of power within them will vary according to the economic climate, the job market and the pace of change. The significance of the contracts is the influence they have on career choices through the expectations of managers about the contractual terms on offer.

Managers these days are less likely than those in the previous generation to automatically pursue a career of hierarchical progression and may choose to move into new types of semi-autonomous organizations, become freelance project managers or consultants, remain at a middle management level or 'downshift' to take up a new, simpler way of life. These changes flow from a desire to achieve the most satisfactory life position and to ensure their psychological and emotional needs are met.

A satisfactory position for both manager and employer is a balanced contract which addresses the needs and interest of both parties. Managers need to consider carefully how and where they are likely to find the most satisfactory contract to meet their specific needs and what they have to offer to an employer in exchange. Herriot and Pemberton (1992, p. 5) point out that:

> Organisations want to make use of people, but they are often unaware of what people want for themselves. They expect commitment and performance, and they think they can engineer it with performance-related pay and other material inducements. What they don't realise is that it is individuals with whom they are dealing. Individuals differ in their aspirations: these change during the course of their lives.

MAKING CHOICES

The nature of the contract on offer, both its real and perceived nature, and the extent to which individuals can influence and negotiate the terms of the contract so that they meet their requirements is crucial in determining the career choices managers may make, and their satisfaction with the outcome of those choices.

The psychological contract between an employee and an organization reflects the underlying organizational values and assumptions. These values and assumptions indicate the sort of behaviour that is likely to be rewarded with advancement within the organization. Those who exhibit the attributes that the organization values are likely to succeed in moving into more senior roles and are likely to feel comfortable in these positions. Those who do not obviously embody these attributes are less likely to progress, may feel very uncomfortable in more senior roles and receive less recognition than their peers, however effective they may be in their work role. One manager commented that behaviour which had once been accepted and valued became unacceptable as the values and management style of the organization changed, resulting in feelings of alienation and rejection. This was the point at which he chose to leave the organization.

Before competing for senior management posts it is worth managers researching the values and assumptions of the organization and considering whether this is an environment in which they are likely to achieve a psychological contract which will meet their own needs.

The psychological contract is also influenced by the nature of each individual's 'career anchors'. These are defined by Schein (1985, p. 127) as 'the pattern of self-perceived talents, motives and values ... [that] serves to guide, constrain, stabilise, and integrate the person's career'.

The five career anchors set out in Schein's model are now examined.

TECHNICAL/FUNCTIONAL COMPETENCE

Individuals with this career anchor value their professional competence and are likely to want to stay in an environment where they can continue to utilize and develop their skills. They may therefore be reluctant to move into roles with broader responsibilities or at a managerial level which makes them remote from direct contact with the professional area of their work.

The experience of senior managers interviewed for this chapter is that their roles have changed substantially since they were first appointed to their posts and that this has included increased responsibility and a broader remit so that they are often managing areas in which they have no professional background or training. The speed of organizational change means that this trend is likely to continue and managers who wish to remain within a particular professional discipline may need to look for career progression in other directions.

The challenge for individuals with this focus and for their employers is to identify roles which enable them to continue to develop and add value while remaining in a particular work area. Managers may need to consider working outside an organization on a freelance or consultancy basis in order to continue to achieve the right level of stimulation and challenge within their field. They will also need to continually monitor the changing needs of organizations and update their professional skills in line with those needs in order to retain their position as technical specialists.

Managers with this career anchor may choose to meet some of their psychological and emotional needs through activity within their professional sphere and become acknowledged leaders in a particular specialism at a regional or national level. This may result in individuals meeting their needs for recognition, status and authority at a level which is not attainable within their employment.

MANAGERIAL COMPETENCE

Individuals with this career anchor value their managerial rather than their professional competence and look for the opportunity to exercise responsibility and contribute to the achievement of organizational goals. This is the key career anchor of many of the senior managers interviewed who expected their jobs to require leadership, political, strategic planning and financial and human resource management skills. The reasons these managers gave for choosing to move into their current jobs and management roles included, 'because I thought I had something to contribute', 'I wanted to influence how services developed and make a difference', 'I wanted to be in a position to do things the way I wanted to do them'.

SECURITY AND STABILITY

Those for whom security and stability is a key career anchor value continuity and may be challenged by the current managerial environment as the rate of organizational change means that there is little stability and security in managerial posts. One manager described the apparent expendability of staff at senior levels as 'chilling'.

It would appear that managers need to recognize that in this environment their sense of security has to come from within and be a product of their own self-awareness, confidence and self-esteem rather than something which results from their position in an organization.

CREATIVITY

Managers for whom creativity is a key anchor seem more likely to reject a conventional senior management role or only take on such roles where a favourable contract can be negotiated. Some managers with this 'anchor' have chosen to take on short-term development projects or look for secondment opportunities with scope for innovation and creative freedom. There may be scope for creativity in an organization which is restructuring and downsizing but this needs to be clearly identified and the desire of the manager to focus in this way needs to be explicitly recognized.

AUTONOMY AND INDEPENDENCE

Managers for whom autonomy and independence are key drivers may find themselves uncomfortable in large organizations, particularly public service ones, because of the move towards centralized planning and performance management. Managers with autonomy and independence as a prime career anchor may be drawn to freelance and consultancy work or become senior managers in small agencies where they have substantial control over strategic and operational decisions and their personal goals and work pattern.

CHOICE AND LIFE STAGE

The key career anchor for each individual manager will be different and may not be constant throughout their life, changing in relation to their career and life stage and to major life events. Careers can be characterized as going through various phases which can be linked to life stages. Herriot (1992) describes the model set out by

Arthur and Kram in which they suggest three main stages, exploring, directedness and protecting.

- Exploring – may last until the early to mid 30s. In this stage, individuals are developing their competence at their jobs, and forming occupational identities. They learn a lot by doing, especially by performing technical or functional tasks, and often demonstrate energy and enthusiasm.
- Directedness – Individuals have become clear about some career anchors. The career anchor of managerial competence may well gain preference over technical and functional competence for many people at this stage.
- Protecting state – after their mid to late 40s, people need to secure and maintain their status, experience continual affirmation of their work and pass on the benefits of their learning and experience to others.

The needs associated with the protecting state are perhaps the most unlikely to be met within the current organizational environment where there is often a lack of respect for experience or length of service. It is the difficulty of negotiating an acceptable psychological contract to meet the needs at this stage that is one of the factors in causing senior managers to seek early retirement.

Decisions about whether to apply for a senior management post, take a year off and go round the world, become a consultant or move into a smaller, more flexible organization will be influenced by an individual manager's key career anchor, their view of what the psychological contract might be in these situations, their life stage, their aspirations, their level of self-awareness and self-esteem and their view of their work life/balance. One senior manager took the opportunity to take early retirement because his key career anchor had become security and stability: retirement and regular income from a pension gave him more certainty of this than continuing within the organization. He had reached the 'protecting state' and felt that the organization did not recognize his potential contribution or value his experience and he was concerned that his life/work balance was having an adverse effect on his family and wished to change this.

Another manager at the directedness stage, with the career anchors of creativity and autonomy and independence opted to move out of a large public sector organization into a job with a less secure short-term contract in a smaller, more flexible agency where there was more opportunity for initiative, innovation, and personal power and control.

THE CHALLENGE OF SENIOR MANAGEMENT

The momentum for a manager to make a career or life change may come from internal or external pressures.

One response to the rapidly changing demands and pressures on organizations has been repeated restructuring driven by the quest to drive down costs, create a smaller, more productive workforce and respond to customer, market or government pressures. This has meant the creation of new jobs with new requirements.

These events have provided some managers with enormous opportunities to take on jobs which have been stimulating and rewarding. Existing managers have sometimes, however, not been perceived by the organizations to have the skills necessary for these roles or have not wished to take on new roles available to them. Managers in these situations face the choice of moving into new posts with new responsibilities and skill requirements or leaving the organization voluntarily or compulsorily.

This can mean individuals moving into managerial posts they might not have chosen to apply for under other circumstances. The impact of a poor 'fit' between the manager and an enforced new role can lead to feelings of inadequacy and lack of confidence: managers in this situation might consider ways of improving the psychological contract or look at other measures to limit the negative impact of their work situation in order to prevent their competence being undermined. This is a point at which levels of personal confidence and self-esteem are critical.

CHALLENGES AND RESOURCES

The level of challenge presented by a job and the internal and external resources available to a manager to meet that challenge are an integral part of the psychological contract. Some managers have chosen not to take up posts, or to leave them, when the perceived mismatch between the challenge and the resources has been so great as to make it impossible to meet the requirements of the post. The impact of this has been clear in the lack of applicants for more challenging service head posts in organizations where there is no apparent framework for support, development or establishing priorities.

Some of the internal resources identified by managers as necessary to operate effectively in senior management roles were stamina, determination, independence, self-reliance, confidence, flexibility, capacity for hard work, a survival instinct and the ability to put work in perspective. The potential for feeling isolated and being caught between the competing demands of customers, staff and boards or political committees were also highlighted as pressures which individuals needed to be equipped to respond to.

The external resources and support valued by these managers included friends, membership of a peer group, access to training and the opportunity to develop new skills, recognition of achievement, mentoring, and support from corporate management. The development of new skills appears to be a particular contributor to both managers' satisfaction with their position and support in difficult times, partly because of the sense of progression and achievement but also as a source of contact with a peer group and a possible temporary escape to a less challenging environment on a training course or conference.

The impact of the relationship between challenge and available resources is indicated by the grid below. There was a general assumption amongst the managers interviewed that senior management posts would be high challenge but that the strain of being in a place where the level of challenge was not matched by resources was not sustainable for long periods. Clearly the level of challenge fluctuates over time but the internal resources of managers also become depleted and more external support is then required if the challenge/resource balance is to be maintained. Managers found that life was most difficult when the external support was reduced and challenge increased in other areas of life due, for example, to the illness of partner or friend.

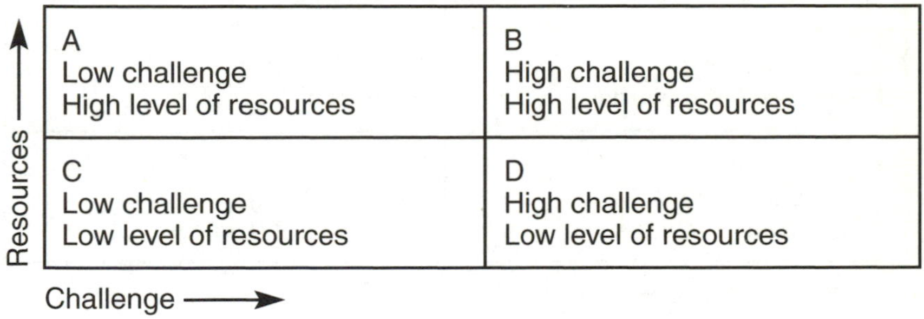

	A Low challenge High level of resources	B High challenge High level of resources
Resources ↑	C Low challenge Low level of resources	D High challenge Low level of resources
	Challenge ⟶	

Figure 8.1   Challenge/resources grid

Managers have chosen to leave posts where the gap between the challenge and the resources available has been too wide to be tolerable. In order to bridge this gap, managers should be aware of the balance between the current level of challenge facing them and their resources.

Where managers feel that their internal resources are insufficient as a result of the demands of their role they may need to explore ways of increasing their external support. This may be through support from a line manager, mentoring, membership of an action learning set or networks of friends and colleagues.

CHALLENGES AND REWARDS

A prevalent perception of the current experience of senior managers is that they work long hours, managing an impossible workload, pressurized by conflicting and impossible demands, sacrificing their family and social life with very little recognition or reward. Potential senior managers are concerned by what appears to be the all-consuming nature of these roles and whether the rewards truly reflect the level of commitment required.

There is a clear expectation that the size of the challenge presented by a job should be matched by the reward. These rewards may be financial or more intangible, such as opportunities for personal development and growth.

Some managers at second-tier level have commented that they would not be interested in a post at first-tier level because the financial rewards would not balance the additional challenge. Senior managers in post have suggested that, while financial rewards may be important to them, their primary motivation is the opportunity for personal growth and development, to make a contribution to the service and to derive a sense of achievement.

The relationship between challenge and reward is indicated by the grid below.

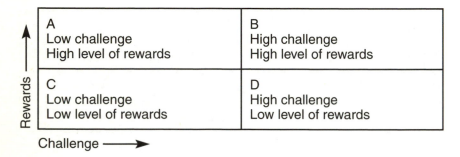

Figure 8.2   Challenge/rewards grid

Expectations of levels of challenge, reward and resources or support have a major impact on whether individuals consider a career move into a more senior post. There is a mismatch between the perceptions of those considering such a move and those who have experienced a senior management role. Every senior manager interviewed felt that, whatever the level of challenge they had faced, the experience had been beneficial and that they would make the same choice again.

IMPLICATIONS FOR CAREER MANAGEMENT

One of the key implications of the discussion above for making effective career choices is the necessity of self-awareness and evaluation and understanding of the organizational environment. The negotiation of a satisfactory psychological contract is dependent on an individual manager's clarity about their life goals and current needs and their value to the organization. It is important for a manager to identify whether their contribution is crucial or important but non-essential, and to appreciate the strengths and weakness of their own position and that of the organization (Herriot and

Pemberton, 1995). A manager's confidence in their own self-worth and the value they can add is critical. Senior managers expressed the view that 'I need to feel that the job needs me more than I need the job' and 'if I had known I could survive outside an organization, I would have been freer to operate within it and that would have been empowering'.

One source of confidence and self-esteem for managers is the mix of skills and experience they bring. The new environment in which managers operate emphasizes individual responsibility for self-development and the construction of a portfolio of skills. These skills and competencies have been explored in detail in Chapter 5. Self-development is an ongoing process which flows from individual life goals and is planned, controlled and evaluated by individuals themselves. It is directly linked to the need for self-assessment and awareness and an analysis of personal strengths and development needs in relation to job or life roles that an individual may aspire to. Chapter 4 explores some of the qualities and characteristics which may need to be analysed. Self-development activities contribute to an individual's career portfolio and it is this portfolio that indicates the value that a manager can bring to an organizational or life role. In making career choices managers should take into account the opportunities provided for self-development and the expansion of their portfolio. Senior managers emphasized the opportunities for self-development as one of the main rewards of their roles and individuals should evaluate such posts in terms of the key management skills that they may develop and enhance. Opportunities to gain substantial budgetary and human resource management experience may, for example, be available in posts at lower levels in the public sector than the private sector and these posts could provide valuable career moves for managers wishing to add these skills to their portfolio.

The nature of a manager's portfolio may change over time in response to their career choices and assessment of the requirements of their future life roles both in work and outside.

CONFIDENCE, SELF-ESTEEM AND FEELING VALUED

A persistent theme raised in discussions with managers is their loss of a sense of being valued by the organization. A number of managers commented that they felt less valued than they had been when they first took on their current roles and that they had stopped expecting any appreciation or recognition. This change may reflect the transition from relational to transactional contracts.

The recognition of their contribution and status in an organization has for some managers been the source of their self-confidence and esteem. If this recognition and appreciation is no longer available then managers must find other means of sustaining their sense of self-worth. This may come partly through their self-assessment of the value of what they have to offer to the organization or from their roles outside work, and managers may need to actively consider how they can develop and maintain their confidence.

In the new transactional contracting situation, confidence and a sense of self-worth are part of the attributes that an individual brings to the organization and are essential requirements for the negotiation of a satisfactory, balanced contract.

LIFE/WORK BALANCE

A major reason for managers choosing to leave jobs or not to move into more demanding roles is the impact on their life/work balance.

All managers perceived or experienced senior management roles to be demanding and to require long hours and a more significant workload. Managers in post identified difficulties in maintaining a satisfactory life/work balance and described not having as much free time as they would like, taking anxieties home, re-arranging home life round work and continually choosing between family and work demands and regularly feeling that they did not meet either satisfactorily. The pressures of having a young family and managing a demanding full-time job led one potential senior manager to take a career break and to negotiate a part-time contract with her employer for the future. This manager had taken maternity leave when having her two children and had no doubt that this had affected her promotion prospects and had passed up the opportunity to apply for a more senior post because she was not prepared to work the hours necessary. She commented that before she had had a family her life/work balance had been very different and this had been acceptable because work then had been the centre of her life and her work colleagues had also provided her main social network.

Life/work balance issues can lead managers to explore opportunities for career breaks or early retirement or to become self-employed and take on consultancy or project work or to consider radical changes in their lifestyle.

The term 'downshifting' has been used to describe the choice to switch to a less stressful job, to work part-time or from home or to negotiate new working arrangements with an employer which provide more freedom and control. The motivation for downshifting is to gain control of life, to find a better balance between work and life outside work and improve the quality of life. It may also be due to a desire for a simpler more sustainable lifestyle with less emphasis on the acquisition of consumer goods and a focus on the spiritual side of life. Downshifting is seen as a route to finding more time for family and friends and the pursuit of personal interests. Downshifting can be a permanent or temporary state and may be part of a new career pattern which addresses the life/work balance by interspersing periods of intensive work with periods without work which create opportunities to focus on other aspects of life.

CONCLUSION

The discussion above has outlined the nature of the psychological contract between managers and their employing organizations, some of the issues which impact on the employee side of that contract, and the way individuals managers can prepare themselves for entering these contracts.

An analysis based on these factors may lead an individual to choose to move into a senior management post or to take another career path because the reality of a senior management role will not meet their psychological and emotional needs, because the implications for their life/work balance are not what they want or because they do not feel that their mix of skills and experience and characteristics would enable them to feel comfortable in, or meet the demands of, such a post.

The nature of the relationship between employees and their employing organizations has changed substantially in the last twenty years. The nature of management careers has also changed in response to the same pressures and in making choices about the future of their careers managers need to:

- be clear about the contract they wish to enter into with an employer
- know what they have to contribute to a job and want they want to gain from it
- be prepared to leave the job and move on when that psychological contract ceases to add value
- be confident and have self-esteem which is vested in a realistic assessment of their own value, rather than confidence and security provided by their place within an organization
- be prepared to develop a portfolio of skills which are designed to prepare them for the likely requirements of their roles in work, and life outside work, in the future.

NOTE

1   http://www.wrdi-institute.com/content/11_FAQs/11_C_Page_004.htm

9 Case studies

In speaking of lies, we come inevitably to the subject of truth. There is nothing simple or easy about this idea. There is no 'the truth', 'a truth' – truth is not one thing, or even a system. It is an increasing complexity. The pattern of the carpet is the surface. When we look closely, or when we become weavers, we learn of the tiny multiple threads unseen in the overall pattern, the knots on the underside of the carpet.

Excerpt from 'Women and honor: some notes on lying', from *Arts of the Possible: Essays and Conversations*, by Adrienne Rich. Copyright 2001 by Adrienne Rich. Used by permission of the author and W.W. Norton and Company, Inc.

INTRODUCTION

The following case studies are intended to illuminate the theories and concepts outlined in the preceding chapters. Using a mix of real-life examples they bring together examples of the ways in which life experiences and feelings influence career choice and career development.

Some of these choices and decisions are clear, and the individuals chosen indicate that internal events have a clear causal effect on external choices, behaviours and development. Some of the exemplars are very aware of their motivations and patterns of behaviour, while others struggle much harder to make sense of what are seemingly unrelated issues. The patterns and feelings are processed internally, and this can happen in a positive way as a result of early nurture, clear self-awareness, good support systems, or organizational support. Professional support has also been utilized in some cases, again depending on the extent of personal awareness. Clear decisions have been made, and choices acted upon. Conversely, others struggle to make sense of work and career if some of these factors have been lacking.

For others, career development can be seen to be a pragmatic process of making some kind of sense out of longings and ideals which are not perceived by family or peer group as logical or appropriate, but which relate to their earlier experiences. This acting out of phantasies can affect early choices, such as working in an environment which is seen as socially or politically unconventional, and which is then utilized in later years in a creative way. Others work in an environment or sector which fits personal aspirations and which also brings together internal needs with external reality – this can be a clear pattern or one which merges with experience to bring career and life satisfaction.

These all have to be considered within their personal, experiential and organizational frameworks, as they provide the main frameworks for each individual story.

RESEARCHER

Jane is currently a freelance consultant and writer, working both within the traditional confines of the LIS professions, and also in the wider organizational arena.

Her current work reflects her career pattern and personal history. Only child of elderly parents, her childhood was a little isolated, and she was left to fend for herself a lot of the time. This made her relatively self-sufficient, but also wary of other children. Her parents had to be supported, and so she also became efficient and, to some extent, controlling, although without recognizing this. The need for other people and support for her was denied, as her own emotional needs were neglected to some extent, and so the world was presented with the façade of a self-sufficient, organized (controlled), and well-behaved child. Beneath this was a strong need to achieve, so that recognition and affection would follow.

The experiences, linked to the need for order and control continued during university education, with law being the unsurprising choice of subject. There was a pattern, an undemanding pattern, and it could all be explained and organized. A bright shiny degree came at the end of it, but not quite bright and shiny enough to lead into prestigious research jobs. So again, a sense of not being good enough, as she had not been good enough for her demanding parents as a small child. The need to be better than the surrounding world became increasingly powerful – rejection can produce anger, and for her this anger was creative.

The degree was, however, very useful. In order to work in the broader research arena, she realized that what she could do was, in fact, to support researchers and practitioners, via the identification and location of information. To do this carefully, and sometimes brilliantly, was then a more useful or powerful tool than just being a boring researcher – it involved lateral thinking, working on search relationships, and pursuing hunches in relation to information retrieval. At the same time information needed to be controlled, and the searches needed to be controlled, but creativity was also important. Carrying out this process well was a victory over the researchers – she was better and more clever than they were but, at the same time, she was also operating in their world. At last she was good enough and received the approval and praise which had so far been denied her.

Logic and ambition then determined a postgraduate diploma, with information science being the obvious choice. More and more information work in more and more specific legal areas followed, so that her specialism in this particular field led to increasing demand. Good information scientists were in woefully short supply, and so to some extent she could choose her own style and place of working.

Efficiency, flair and a nose for developing areas of interest led into being asked to carry out particular projects for some of the major drug companies. This market niche was then further developed through offering consultancy on how the information function in specific companies could be developed and contribute to overall profit making. The role provided status, she was in control of what she did and when, there were good financial rewards, and the presentation of reports provided a satisfactory end product, both for her and for the companies involved.

This has now developed into an information consultancy function in other corporate organizations, with the pharmaceutical companies providing the bulk of her work, and has enabled her to build up a satisfying career that closely relates to her inner world and life experiences.

TEACHER, RESEARCHER AND WRITER

Family dynamics and a need for a place and materials which supported her phantasies led Jean into the world of librarianship in the public sector. But this beginning did not follow the standard pattern of small steps up the career ladder, and then bigger steps to the top; instead it led into research, teaching and training.

The family was traditional, conservative, and found it difficult to collectively or individually express any emotions. Of the four siblings, Jean was the youngest, with the three older siblings already established within the family system when she was born. The birth order probably had a strong effect on her, as there was insufficient time to be given to her real needs, and so compensate for the lack of family affection and activities: in the time-honoured way, she discovered the world of books. Phantasies were lived out and experienced through reading – anywhere, anytime and almost anything.

The phantasies also fed her own ideas about work and careers. Instead of following the accepted family norms and values of 'safe' and 'good' work, such as secretarial work, nursing, teaching, or being a nanny, she was determined to enter the world of librarianship and make a success of it. That world included resources unlimited and could maybe satisfy both her and others. It gave her direct access to those resources which fed her own phantasies. Defying the family, she became qualified, worked in the public sector, and became an efficient and caring manager, thus achieving status; at the same time she became independent of the family to a large extent.

Her work enabled her to some extent to open up her phantasies to the rest of the world, in the sense of providing a good service to the public, but one which involved imagination, initiative, and resources that could support the secret world of many readers.

Because of her genuine interest in the subject and in the provision of wide-ranging resources in a flexible setting in the public sector, she then became involved in part-time teaching, so linking the practical and theoretical aspects of the profession. This was immensely satisfying, as her own ideas could be given to students, at the stage when they were enthusiastic and willing to take on new concepts. At the same time, there was interest in the public sector in general in the expectations of the users, and the ways in which they used services in relation to their own ideals. This interest and need for customer feedback linked with the way in which the sector was trying to establish patterns of use between personal reading habits and resource provision, using research methodology. It provided an alternative approach, rather than continuing the traditional professional system of resource provision, based on 'professional' expertise. It also provided a supportive framework.

The combination of research and teaching was too much to resist, combined with the desire to spread her ideas more widely. So the next logical step was to move into full-time teaching, but also continue with the valuable and recognized research. At the same time her considerable experience enabled her to achieve recognition with a major professional publishing company, and several writing contracts followed. This satisfied her need to use her original ideas, to communicate them, and not to be locked into a pre-determined pattern of behaviour as required to some extent by her family. It also gave her professional status, and from this she could choose to move into part-time teaching, part-time research and part-time writing.

Using experience and transferable skills she was able to develop a flexible career portfolio which contributed to professional development in the widest sense, and also satisfied her own psychological needs.

TRAINER

Born into an affectionate and stable family, Bryan was the oldest of three siblings. He was aged five when his younger sister was born, and this had a strong impact on him. His place as the most important member of the family had been usurped, and he was convinced that his sister now had pride of place, and that he was not so important.

He began to work out strategies to gain back the attention which he felt he had lost, and particularly his close relationship with his father. These strategies were, of course, not clearly defined in his head at this age, but the feelings were very strong, and he remembers them clearly now. A major element was the need to achieve, and so be close again to his father. This meant reading as many books as possible that belonged to his scientist father, starting at this very young age with father's own childhood books, but continuing to read whatever he understood until mid-career. Internalizing these feelings and ideas was very important to establish himself as part of his own growing up. At the same time his mother encouraged him to read and look at books, and used to sit with him and look at picture books, at art reproductions and travel scenes, even before he went to school. She continued to do this with his sister, but these early memories of books and, especially, pictures are precious to him.

Another key memory is that of the neighbour whose house was full of books, where peace and quiet reigned, and where books could be read for hours at a time – books that were fun, or childish, or full of clever exploits. He longed to take some of them away, as they were as delicious as sweets, but was scared to do this, and could not ask if he could borrow any of them. But he did 'borrow' a postcard from the neighbour's postcard collection, showing a wonderful scene: this symbolized his jealousy and envy of this neighbour and the book collection, and enabled him to take this token away with him.

His sister had a clear niche in the household, but he still had to find his. Reading and reading well and fast seemed one way of doing this. Piles of books were read, others were borrowed from classmates at school, and walking around with books that had been read and absorbed indicated achievement. 'This is what I can do, and I can do it well and quickly' – so approval would follow. The phantasy was that the books themselves would lead to this much-needed approval.

School was followed by university, because that was what was expected, but rather than attending a radical art college, reflecting those earlier pictures, he accepted a place on a more traditional degree course – this was what the family expected, and so that was what he had to do. Further study at Master's level proved to be difficult at this stage, and so he again followed the traditional route and went into teaching. This was not the ideal choice, and so a postgraduate diploma in library and information studies was an obvious alternative, linking up with the 'I have always loved books' emotions. After qualifying, working as a classifier was intellectually satisfying at one level, but not at another – there was no time to explore and enjoy the books that were being added to the large and good academic collection, so this felt frustrating.

However, as the organization was in a state of change, there were opportunities for promotion, and a step up the ladder. Having responsibility for other people was a positive and rewarding step, and when a further promotion presented itself, training within the library context, he applied for and got this. This led to a series of increasingly senior posts, all with a major training and personnel component, but all set within library services. The next logical step was to train in the personnel field, and then take a Master's course in personnel development – this was finally achieved, and approval gained. A course in coaching followed, and led to a senior post in a large county authority, where libraries were the core business of the division, but people and development were his specific responsibility.

Bryan now feels that he has achieved some kind of status, and is able to assert himself as a person and establish his identity within the county. He no longer has to strive to be recognized by his father. His confidence is clear, and he has a sense of having 'found' his place in the career structure within a defined organization. The path may have been complex, but he is clear now that he has found it.

PROJECT MANAGER

Barbara is in her early thirties, lives alone, and has a sister who is severely disabled and who is several years younger than her. Both parents are alive, but quite distant in both geographical and emotional terms. The younger sister is cared for within a specialist organization.

Barbara is a senior manager with overall responsibility for information systems in a large, highly structured blue-chip company. She is currently discussing her future with the employee counsellor in the company, as she is at a crossroads, and is unsure in which direction her career should progress. This is perplexing her, as she was appointed to this very senior position at a very young age, as a result of her drive and initiative within the company. She is fully aware of the potential of knowledge management, and has the appropriate background and experience. However, in the context of fee earning and maximizing resources, it is not possible for her to 'coast' along, and she is being pressured to apply for a secondment to study for a full-time MBA. This would then open up new career opportunities, but the downside is that it would tie her to the company for two years.

Her difficulty is that taking the MBA would move her out of her own 'comfort zone', and present a considerable and personal challenge. She finds this uncomfortable, as she has been with the company since graduating, knows how it operates, and feels familiar with its ethos and parameters. Also she is popular with the members of her team, feels supported by them, and has encouraged others to qualify in the information field. She has also encouraged her staff to develop, and has been on several short courses on mentoring.

She has achieved status and satisfaction, but at some cost. She lives alone, puts all her efforts into her work and into the company, and the company and her colleagues represent her family and her social life. To leave all this and take a huge risk feels difficult and dangerous. At the same time she is fully aware of the need to achieve, and to support the market philosophy of the company.

She feels that it would be difficult to separate from the company, and is also somewhat apprehensive of being measured elsewhere, in this case on the MBA course, and not being perfect, or even good enough. The new environment and demands feel persecutory, even before she has started the course, hence her hesitation.

After talking about her difficulties and fears with the human resource division, she became clearer in her own mind about the difficulties that she was facing, real and imagined. This exploration led to an interim solution; secondment to a sister company for three months to set up a knowledge management network there, which would then be reviewed at the end of the three months. If the foundations were laid, and she and management were satisfied, then she could continue for another three months. After this, she would return to the parent company. Chief Knowledge Officer status and salary were the rewards offered.

This solution gave her time to try out new fields, but using her existing information skills, while not being separated from the situation that she knew and liked. If the interim separation worked, then she would be more able to tackle the MBA, return, and then probably move to a more senior post within the company. She could then move on to another company if an opportunity arose at the right time.

Understanding her own dilemmas and talking them through enabled her to make a good career development decision, opening up the way to further opportunities. If she had been pressured, then it would have been very difficult for her to adjust to a new set of circumstances. The company acted in a very containing way – partly as a result of company policy, and partly in recognition of talent that needed to be nurtured in the face of fierce national and global competition.

PART-TIME MANAGER – VOLUNTARY SECTOR LIBRARY

Joan was the oldest child of parents representing two cultures. Her father came from the Caribbean and her mother from Ireland, and the family lived and grew up in London. Her feelings of being overwhelmed as a child have constantly re-surfaced as an adult, and have been reflected in her work patterns and emotional responses to stress.

She was the oldest of four siblings – the next sibling was a sister, and then almost immediately boy twins were born into the family. Resources were scarce, the house was small, and although her father was a lawyer and clever, he was never able to earn sufficient money to enable to the family to feel comfortable – everything was scarce. To help the household finances, her mother sometimes worked night shifts in the local hospital, leaving the care of the children to Joan. Her father found childcare difficult and tedious and often divested himself of these responsibilities in many ways.

Growing up was overwhelming at times – there was never enough space in the small house for all the children, never enough time to attend to all their needs, and never enough attention from either parent. Father was pre-occupied with work and financial difficulties, and her mother was tired from constantly juggling demands with insufficient resources.

However, the family held strong political and religious views; Joan was brought up as a Catholic but rejected this in her teens. She went to university and obtained a degree which combined politics with economics – this in some ways fitted in with the discussions and interests of the family. But it was insufficient to enable her to get a job; she did not want to teach, and so instead decided to train as an information worker, so that she could obtain a post in an organization which reflected her own political and sociological views.

She first worked in a university library, as an assistant, but found this stifling. She then moved to the corporate sector, filled with reforming zeal, but realized that this environment was not for her. These posts were full-time, but she was finding them stressful in relation to all the other activities that she was involved in – community work, political work and sharing ideas with her friends. Keeping on top of it all, and maintaining some semblance of order in her private life at home, such as cooking and cleaning, began to be too much for her.

As life as a small child had overwhelmed her, she had begun to create the same atmosphere around her as an adult. But she talked about this with her manager at work, and began to realize what was happening. Making space for herself as well as for work was the answer, and so working part-time, in an environment with which she could identify, seemed positive. She created a style of work that was divided into chunks, but all of them manageable, rather than overwhelming.

With the expansion of work and the increasing importance of information in the political and voluntary sectors, she is assured of work, but has no wish to climb further up the career ladder. Finding a way of working that allows space for herself is ideal, and she may move around to other services in the sector that are of interest to her, but is clear that more responsibility is not for her. Working through the ways in which her adult life reflected her earlier experiences has been invaluable, and led to a balanced style of operating.

LOCAL STUDIES LIBRARIAN

Ian has always been interested in history, and his family were involved in many of the local activities in the village where he was brought up. He has one sister, and they and his parents are very close. His father is a teacher, and his mother works part-time as a nurse.

His love of maps, books and artefacts led naturally into a career in librarianship, and to specializing in local history. He decided not to go to university, but to take an external degree in library and information studies, and to specialize in local history studies in his placements and project. After a couple of junior posts in the public sector, he is now in charge of the collection in the central library of a local authority – not a very senior post, but one that is unique. It deals only with one geographical area, but is an excellent collection and well used by researchers and students as well as members of the public. He is paid to do what he loves and does best, and is happy being within a fairly traditional structure. It reflects the strong family structure in which he grew up. Organization, innovation and care for the job make the match between the individual and the job ideal.

This post will not become outdated for him, as maintaining the collection and thinking about its maximum use will continue to be of value and interest. It is also part of the ethos of the local authority – supporting local history and its environments.

STATISTICIAN/INFORMATION WORKER

The youngest of three siblings, Susan's career has been interesting and varied. She is now a senior member of a research team in a large county, concerned with providing housing and services to the elderly.

It suits her and her talents, but has not been a traditional route to satisfaction. She did well at school, and was spurred on by her two elder siblings who were high achievers, particularly the ambitious and very clever older brother. He was always ahead in everything, and she has vivid memories of trying to catch up with him both physically and mentally as a child. He became an outstanding surgeon, and so rather than compete with him in the field of medicine, Susan read economics at university. This suited her, as it was both contained within a clear framework, but also allowed some personal interpretation and innovation.

Rather than teach, she pursued a postgraduate diploma in information studies, having used the university library extensively, and thoroughly enjoyed the process of managing information. This was followed by a couple of years in a university library, using both her subject expertise and information qualification. Several promotions followed, and these were good experiences, and also opened the door to gain some expertise in managing staff in a large organization.

She was then asked to edit some journal articles in the field, and discovered that she also had a gift for proof-reading and editing, and could turn raw material into a sophisticated finished product. This led into work with an academic publisher, and the interest developed to include producing and using statistical information for some of the publications. This was an important experience, as it gave her a specific area of expertise, which was comparatively rare among her peers, and was very useful in the job market. When the post was advertised for the manager of the statistics and information centre in a large county, this was an obvious move. She applied for the post, and was successful.

Now she has job satisfaction and a good standard of living, and is recognized for her expertise in her own right, and has no need to fight to leave the shadow of her high-achieving brother. It also gives her a good jumping-off ground to move into other more senior posts in local government.

Appendix 1:
Useful organizations and websites

Advancing Women	http://www.advancingwomen.com/services.html
Advisory, Conciliation and Arbitration Services	http://www.acas.org.uk/
Aslib	http://www.aslib.co.uk/
Association for Coaching	http://www.associationforcoaching.com/
Association of Graduate Careers Advisory Services	http://www.agcas.org.uk/
Association of Graduate Recruiters	http://www.agr.org.uk/
British Association for Counselling and Psychotherapy	http://www.bacp.co.uk/
British Computer Society	www1.bcs.org.uk/bm/
British Council	http://www.britishcouncil.org/
British Executive Service Overseas	http://www.beso.org/
British Psychological Society	http://www.bps.org.uk/
Capita RAS (Recruitment Advisory Services)	http://www.capitas.co.uk/
Career Coaching – Waring Well	http://www.waringwell.com/
Career Counselling Services	http://www.career-counselling-services.co.uk/
Career Development Group	http://www.careerdevelopmentgroup.org.uk/
Career Development Guide	http://www.placementmanual.com/
Career Energy	http://www.careerenergy.co.uk/
Career Potential	http://www.careerpotential.co.uk/
Careers Europe	http://www.careerseurope.co.uk/
Careers Research and Advisory Centre	http://www.kellysearch.com/
Centre for Career Management	http://www.centreforcareermanagement.com/

Centre for Coaching	http://www.centreforcoaching.com/
Centre for Guidance Studies	http://www.derby.ac.uk/cegs/
Centre for Stress Management	http://www.managing stress.com/
Chartered Institute of Library and Information Professionals	http://www.lisjobnet.org.uk/
Chartered Institute of Personnel and Development	http://www.cipd.co.uk/
City and Guilds	http://www.city-and-guilds.co.uk/
Coaching Academy	http://www.thecoachingacademy.com/
Coaching and Mentoring Network	http://www.coachingnetwork.org.uk/
Commission for Racial Equality	http://www.cre.gov.uk/
Confederation of British Industry	http://www.cbi.org.uk/
Connexions Partnership	http//www.connexions.gov.uk/
Council for Excellence in Management and Leadership	http://www.managementandleadershipcouncil.org/
Cultural Heritage National Training Organisation (CHNTO)	http://www.chnto.co.uk/
DCMS Wolfson Grant Programme	http://www.culture.gov.uk/heritage/wolfson/
Department for Education and Skills	http://www.dfes.gov.uk/europeopen/
Disability Portfolio	http://www.resource.gov.uk/action/learnacc/00access_03.asp
Disabled Living Foundation	http://www.dlf.org.uk/
Equal Opportunities Commission	http://www.eoc.org.uk/
European Mentoring Centre	http://www.emccouncil.org/
Glass Ceiling	http://www.theglassceiling.com/
Glen Recruitment	http://www.glenrecruitment.co.uk/
Graduate Career Information Advisory Services	http://www.prospects.ac.uk/
HIMSS	http://www.himss.bham.ac.uk/
INFOmatch Recruitment Agency	http://www.infomatch@cilip.org.uk/

Information Services National Training Organisation (isNTO)	http://www.isnto.org.uk/
Instant Library Recruitment	http://www.instant-library.com/
Institute of Career Guidance	http://www.icg-uk.org/
Institute of Directors	http://www.iod.co.uk/
Institute of Group Analysis	http://www.igalondon.org.uk/
Institute of Management	http://www.imc.co.uk/
Institute of Work Psychology	http://www.shef.ac.uk/niwp/
International Career Development Library	http://icdl.uncg.edu/
International Coach Federation	http://www.coachfederation.org/
International Federation of Library Associations	http://www.ifla.com/
International Foundation for Action Learning	http://www.ifal.org.uk/
International Knowledge Management Network	http://www.cibit.com/
Learn Direct	http://www.learndirect.co.uk/
LIBEX (Bureau for International Library Staff Exchange)	http://www.cilip.org.uk/
Library and Information Commission	http://www.lic.gov.uk/news/
Life Coaching Company	http://www.lifecoaching-company.co.uk/
Local Government Agency (LGA)	http://www.lga.gov.uk/
London Graduate Recruitment Fair	http://www.tsnn.net/show_115_313991.htm
Museums, Libraries and Archives Council	http://www.mla.gov.uk/
National Advisory Centre on Careers for Women	http://www.aim25.ac.uk/ogi-bin/search2?collid
National Centre for Volunteering	http://www.volunteering.org.uk/
National Electronic Library for Health	http://www.nelh.nhs.uk/
NHS Careers: the NHS Team – career option	http://www.nhscareers.nhs.uk/careers/ahp/the_index.html
National Institute for Careers Education and Counselling	http://www.crac.org.uk/

National Literacy Trust (NLT)	http://www.literacytrust.org.uk/about/
National Mentoring Network	http://www.nmn.org.uk/
Central Government National Training Organisation (CGNTO)	http://www.central-gov-nto.org.uk/
National Vocational Qualifications	http://www.dfes.gov.uk/nvq/what.html/
Opportunities for the Disabled	http://www.jobs.irs.gov/Disabled.html/
Oxfam Voluntary Service Council	http://www.oxfam.org.uk/
Professional Coaching Group	http://www.professional-coaching.co.uk/
PULMAN Project	http://www.pulmanweb.org/
Recruit Media Informed	http://www.recruitmedia.co.uk/
Recruitment Employment Federation	http://www.rec.uk.com/
Sector skills councils	http://www.ssda.org.uk/ssc/sscouncil.shtml/
Sector Skills Development Agency	http://www.ssda.org.uk/
Skills Framework for the Information Age	http://www.e-skills.co.uk/sfia
Special Libraries Association (SLA)	http://www.sla.org/
Sue Hill Recruitment and Services Ltd	http://www.tfpl.com
Tavistock and Portman NHS Trust	http://www.tavi-port.org/
The Telework Association	http://www.telework.org.uk/
The Times	http://www.timesonline.co.uk/appointments
The Times Higher Education Supplement	http://www.thesjobs.co.uk/
TRA (Reading Agency)	http://www.readingagency.co.uk/
Unit for the Study of Innovation, Knowledge and Organisational Networks (IKON)	http://users.wbs.warwick.ac.uk/group/ikon/
United Kingdom Council for Psychotherapy	http://www.psychotherapy.org.uk/
UK Jobs Guide	http://www.Ukjobsguide.co.uk
Voluntary Service Overseas	http://www.vso.org.uk/contact/index.htm/
Wannabee.com	http://www.wannabee.com

Wider Information and Library Issues Project	http://www.resource.gov.uk/documents/wilip-rep.pdf http://www.resource.gov.uk/documents/sum.pdf
Work Foundation	http://www.theworkfoundation.com/
Work Life Balance Trust	http://www.w-lb.org.uk/

Appendix 2:
Skills groups and skills sets

These are listed in full in the *TFPL skills toolkit*, London: TFPL, 2003. Detailed descriptors can be found at: http://www.tfpl.com

Personal attributes

Creative/innovative
Entrepreneurial
Assertiveness
Collaborative
Networker
Attention to detail
Leadership skills
Communication
Influencing
Developmental
Team working
Facilitation
Vision

Management and people skills

Organization specific
Planning
Commercial management
Process management
People management
Business development

Core knowledge skills

Knowledge environment/context
Knowledge creation/harvesting
Knowledge capture
Knowledge transfer
Knowledge exploitation
Knowledge processes

Core information skills

Resource management
Information architecture
Research, analysis, advisory services
Dissemination/advisory
Records management

References

Amado, G. and Ambrose, A. (2001) *The Transitional Approach to Change*, London: Karnac.

Arthur, Michael B. and Kram, Kathy E. (1989) 'Reciprocity at work: the separate yet inseparable possibilities for individual and organisational development', in Arthur, Michael B. et al. (eds) *The Handbook of Career Theory*. Cambridge: Cambridge University Press.

BAC (British Association for Counselling) (1993) Information Sheet 1.

Bawden, R. and Zuber-Skerritt, O. (eds.) (2002) 'The concept of process management' in *The Learning Organization*: **9** (3/4).

Bion, W.R. (1961) *Experiences in Groups*, London: Tavistock/Routledge.

Bion, W.R. (1962) *Learning From Experience*, London: Karnac.

Bowlby, J. (1975) *Attachment and Loss, Vol. 2, Separation: Anxiety and Anger*, Harmondsworth: Pelican.

Bowlby, J. (1979) *The Making and Breaking of Affectional Bonds*, London: Tavistock.

Bowlby, J. (1984) *Attachment and Loss, Vol. 1, Attachment*, 2nd edn, Harmondsworth: Pelican.

Centre for Research in Library and Information Management (1997) *Turning Points – Moving into Management*, Preston: Centre for Research in Library and Information Management, University of Central Lancashire.

CILIP (Chartered Institute of Library and Information Professionals) (2002a) 'Giving progress a better chance', *Library and Information Appointments*, **5** (8), p. 1.

CILIP (Chartered Institute of Library and Information Professionals) (2002b) *Revealing the Bigger Picture: Education, Enterprise, Advocacy*. London: CILIP.

CILIP (Chartered Institute of Library and Information Professionals) (2003) *CILIP in the Knowledge Economy: A Leadership Strategy. The Report of the Competitiveness and the Knowledge Based Economy Executive Advisory Group to CILIP.* London: CILIP.

Confederation of British Industry (CBI) (1998) *In Search of Employability: a Discussion Document*, London: CBI.

Corrall, S. (1994) *Personal correspondence.* Cited in Nankivell, C. (2000) 'See your career grow with a mentor', *Library and Information Appointments,* **3** (6), p. 1.

Davidson, M.J. and Cooper, C.L. (1992) *Shattering the Glass Ceiling: The Woman Manager,* London: Paul Chapman.

de Board, R. (1978). *The Psychoanalysis of Organizations,* London: Tavistock.

DCMS (Department for Culture, Media and Sport) (2003) *Framework for the Future,* London: DCMS.

DTI (Department of Trade and Industry) (1998) *Our competitive future: building the knowledge driven economy,* Department of Trade and Industry, White Paper (Cm 4176).

Egan, G. (1998) *The Skilled Helper,* 6th edn, London: Brooks Cole.

Erikson, E. (1950) *Childhood and Society,* New York: Norton.

Freire, P. (1968, 1970) *Pedagogy of the Oppressed,* Seabury. [Reviewed by Leeman, P. on the Freire websites of 2003 created by Schugurensky, D.]

French, R. and Vince, R. (1999) *Group Relations, Management and Organization,* Oxford: Oxford University Press.

Freud, S. (1986) *Historical and Expository Works on Psychoanalysis,* London: Penguin. (Freud Library Vol. 15).

Gabriel, Yiannis (1999) *Organizations in Depth,* London: Sage.

Handy, Charles (1990) *Inside Organisations: 21 Ideas for Managers,* London: BBC Books.

Herriot, Peter (1992) *Career Management Challenge: Balancing Individual and Organisational Needs,* London: Sage.

Herriot, Peter and Pemberton, Carole (1995) *New Deals: The Revolution in Managerial Careers,* Chichester: Wiley.

Hirschhorn, L. (1988) *The Workplace Within: Psychodynamics of Organizational Life,* London: MIT Press.

Hirschhorn, L. (1997) *Reworking Authority: Leading and Following in the Post-Modern Organization,* London: MIT Press.

Holmes, J. (1993) *John Bowlby and Attachment Theory,* London: Routledge.

Huckle, M. (2002) 'Charter still central to CILIP', *Library Association Record,* **104** (2), p. 84.

Hyams, E. (2002) 'Profile of Caroline Plumb', *Library and Information Update,* **1** (9), p. 26.

Ibarra, H. (2002) 'How to stay stuck in the wrong career', *Harvard Business Review,* **80** (12), December, pp. 40–7.

Industrial Society (1996) *Management Fact Sheet: Mentoring,* London: Industrial Society.

Industrial Society (1999) *Managing Best Practice: Coaching,* London: Industrial Society.

Institute of Career Guidance (2001) *A Career in Career Guidance,* Stourbridge: Institute of Career Guidance.

isNTO (Information Services National Training Organisation) (2001) *Skills Foresight in the Information Services Sector: 2000–2007,* London: isNTO.

Kets De Vries, M.F.R. (1995) *Organizational Paradoxes.* 2nd edn, London: Routledge.

Klein, M. (1975) *The Writings of Melanie Klein, Vol. 1, Love, Guilt and Reparation; Vol. 2, Envy and Gratitude and Other Works,* London: Hogarth Press.

Klein, M. (1984) *Our Adult World and Other Essays,* London: Heinemann.

Klein, M. (1987) *Our Need for Others and Its Roots in Infancy,* London: Tavistock.

Law, B. and Watts, A.G. (1977) *Schools, Careers and Community,* London: Church Information Office.

Library Association (2002) *Report of The Policy Advisory Group on a National Information Policy,* London: Library Association.

Lively, P. (1974) *The House in Norham Gardens,* London: Mammoth.

Marris, P. (1974) *Loss and Change,* London: Routledge and Kegan Paul.

Maslow, A. (1994) *The Farther Reaches of Human Behaviour,* London: Penguin.

Maslow, A.H. (1954) *Motivation and Personality,* London: Harper and Row.

Menzies, I.E.P. (1970) *The Functioning of Social Systems as a Defence Against Anxiety,* London: Tavistock.

Morgan, G. (1986) *Images of Organization,* London: Sage.

Myers, I.B. (1993) *Introduction to Type,* 5th edn, Palo Alto: Consulting Psychologists Press.

Nichols, C. (2002/2003) 'Turning Point', *Directions: The Ashridge Journal,* Winter, 2002/2003, pp. 24–6.

Nonaka, I. (1991) 'The knowledge creating company', *Harvard Business Review,* **69** (6) pp. 96–104.

Nonaka, I. and Takeuchi, M. (1995) *The Knowledge Creating Company – How Japanese Companies Create the Dynamics of Innovation,* Oxford: Oxford University Press.

Open Horizons: three scenarios for 2020 (1998) The 1998 report from the Chatham House Forum. London: Royal Institute of International Affairs.

Oshry, B. (1999) *Leading Systems: Lessons from the Power Lab,* San Francisco: Berrett-Koehler.

Parkes, C.M. (1986) *Bereavement: Studies of Grief in Adult Life,* London: Tavistock.

Poland, F., Curran, M. and Owens, R.G. (1995) *Women and Senior Management: A Research Study of Career Barriers and Progression in the Library and Information Sector, Final Report,* London: Library Association.

Renaissance in the Regions: a new vision for England's museums (2001) London, Re:source, The Council for Museums, Archives and Libraries.

Revans, R.W. (1980) *Action Learning; New Techniques for Management,* London, Blond and Briggs.

Roberts, V.Z. (1999) 'Isolation, autonomy, and interdependence in organizational life', in French, R. and Vince, R. *op. cit.*

Rowling, J.K. (2000) *Harry Potter and the Goblet of Fire,* London: Bloomsbury.

Ryle, A.Q. (1990) *Cognitive-analytic Therapy: Active Participation in Change,* Chichester: Wiley.

Sandler, J. (1987) *Projection, Identification, Projective Identification*, London: Karnac.

Sandler, J. et al. (1992) *The Patient and the Analyst*, London: Karnac.

Schein, E.H. (1978) *Career Dynamics: Matching Individual and Organizational Needs*, Reading, Massachusetts: Addison-Wesley.

Schein, E.H. (1985) *Organisational Culture and Leadership*, San Francisco: Jossey-Bass.

Senge, Peter (1994) *The Fifth Discipline: The Art and Practice of the Learning Organization*, London: Century Business (Random House).

Skelton, V. and Abell, A. (2001) *Developing Skills for the Information Services Workforce in the Knowledge Economy. A Report on the Outcomes of Eight Scenario Planning Workshops*, commissioned by the information services National Training Organisation (isNTO), London: TFPL.

Storr, A. (1983) *Jung: Selected Writings*, London: Fontana.

Success Dynamics (2003) *Personality Survey and Job Scan*, Croydon: Success Dynamics International Ltd.

Tamkin, P. and Barber, L. (1998) *Learning to Manage*, The Institute for Employment Studies: Report 345.

Usherwood, Bob et al. (2001) *Recruit, Retain, Lead: The Public Library Workforce Study*, Library and Information Commission Research Report 106. London: Re:source, The Council for Museums, Archives and Libraries.

Waddell, M. (1998) *Inside Lives*, London: Duckworth.

Ward, S. and Abell, A. (2001) *Mobilising Knowledge*: *The Pharmaceutical Industry Approach*, London: P.J.B. Publications Ltd.

Winnicott, D.W. (1965) *The Maturational Processes and the Facilitating Environment*, London: Hogarth Press and the Institute of Psychoanalysis.

Winnicott, D.W. (1971) *Playing and Reality*, Harmondsworth: Penguin.

Bibliography

Abell, A. (1997) *The Information Professional of the 21st Century*, London: TFPL.

Abell, A. and Oxbrow, N. (2001) *Competing with Knowledge: The Information Professional in the Knowledge Management Age*, London: Library Association Publishing.

Apple, M.W. (1996) *Cultural Politics and Education*, Buckingham: Open University Press.

Arnold, J. (1997) *Managing Careers into the 21st Century*, London: Paul Chapman.

Arthur, M.B., Inkson, K. and Pringle, J.K. (1999) *The new careers; individual action and economic change*, London: Sage.

Arundale, J. (1996) *Getting your SNVQ*, London: Library Association Publishing.

Audit Commission (2003) *Building Better Libraries*, London: Audit Commission.

Bion, W.R. (1961) *Experiences in Groups, and Other Papers*, London: Tavistock.

Blosch, M. (1999) 'The new knowledge management supermodel', *Knowledge Management Review*, **8**, pp. 22–5.

Bolles, R. (2003) *Job Hunting on the Internet*, Berkeley: Ten Speed Press.

Bolles, R. (2003) *What Colour is your Parachute?*, Berkeley: Ten Speed Press.

Boreham, J.L. (1967) 'The psychodynamic diagnosis and treatment of vocational problems', *British Journal of Clinical Psychology*, **6**, pp. 150–8.

Bowlby, J. (1969) *Attachment and Loss, Vol. 1, Attachment*, London: Hogarth Press and Institute of Psychoanalysis.

Bowlby, J. (1969) *Attachment and Loss, Vol. 2, Separation: anxiety and anger*, London: Hogarth Press.

Brindley, L. (2002) 'Leadership', *Library and Information Update*, **1** (2), p. 23.

Brine, A. and Beckett, I. (2003) 'A fresh look at CPD', *Library and Information Update* **2** (4), pp. 42–3.

Brown, D. and Brooks, L. (eds) (1996) *Career Choice and Development*, San Francisco: Jossey-Bass.

Bruce, L. and Roberts, S. (2003) 'Job shadowing shaping tomorrow's leaders', *Library and Information Update*, **2** (9) pp. 36–8.

Buchanan, D.A. and Huczynski, A.A. (1985) *Organizational Behaviour*, London: Prentice-Hall.

Burke, M.E. (1992) 'Career development report: one perspective', *Personnel, Training and Education*, **9** (3), pp. 76–7.

'Burn those targets' (2002) *Library and Information Update*, **1** (6), September, p. 8.

Burston, D. (1992) *An A–Z of Careers and Jobs*, London: Kogan Page.

Byrne, D. (2003) 'Mentoring', *Library and Information Update*, **2** (4), pp. 38–9.

Cairncross, F. (2002) *The Company of the Future: Meeting the Management Challenges of the Communications Revolution*, London: Profile Books.

'Career steer award' (2002) *Library and Information Update*, **1** (6), p. 6.

Caruth, D.L. and Hantlogten, G.D. (2000) '11 characteristics of highly effective performance appraisals', *Human Resource Professional*, **13** (1), pp. 12–15.

Cattell, R.G. (1957) *Personality and Motivation Structure and Measurement*, New York: World Books.

Chartered Institute of Library and Information Professionals (CILIP) (2002) *Revealing the Bigger Picture: Education, Enterprise, Advocacy*, London: CILIP.

Chartered Institute of Library and Information Professionals (CILIP) (2003) *CILIP in the Knowledge Economy: A Leadership Strategy: The Report of the Competitiveness and the Knowledge Based Economy Executive Advisory Group to CILIP*, London: CILIP.

Chartered Institute of Library and Information Professionals (CILIP) (2003) *Framework of Qualifications*, London: CILIP.

Chartered Institute of Library and Information Professionals (CILIP) (2005) *Training Directory*, London: CILIP.

Chester, P. (2002) 'A partnership approach', *Career Guidance Today*, **10** (1), pp. 28–9.

Clore Duffield Foundation (2002) *Cultural Leadership: The Clore Leadership Programme*, London: Clore Duffield Foundation.

Clutterbuck, D. (1995) *Everyone Needs a Mentor: Fostering Talent at Work*, 2nd edn, London: Institute of Personnel Management.

Cochran, L. (1997) *Career Counselling: A Narrative Approach*, London: Sage.

Collin, A. and Watts, A.G. (1996) 'The death and transfiguration of career – and career guidance?', *British Journal of Guidance and Counselling*, **24** (3), pp. 385–98.

Collin, A. and Young, R.A. (eds) (2000) *The Future of Career*, Cambridge: Cambridge University Press.

Confederation of British Industry (CBI) (1998) *In Search of Employability: A CBI Discussion Document*, London: CBI.

Conference Board (2000) *Beyond Knowledge Management: New Ways to Work*, by Brian Hackett. London: Conference Board Research Report No. R 1262-00-14.

Corrall, S. (1998) 'Defining professional competence: skills and prospects for the information profession', *State Librarian*, Autumn, pp. 48–63.

Corrall, S. (2003) 'How can our leaders thrive?', *Library and Information Appointments*, **6** (1), pp. 1–2.

Corrall, S., and Brewerton, A. (eds) (1999) 'Personal development', in *The New Professional's Handbook: Your Guide to Information Services Management*, London: Library Association Publishing, pp. 265–93.

Courtney, N. (2003) 'Executive learning: to "e" or not to "e"?' *Library and Information Update*, **2** (2), pp. 36–7.

Dakers, H. (1996) *NVQs and How to Use Them*, London: Kogan Page.

Dalal, F. (2002) *Race, Colour and the Process of Racialization*, London: Brunner-Routledge.

Daley, D.M. (2001) 'Developmental performance appraisal: feedback, interview and disciplinary techniques', *Public Administration and Public Policy*. **19** (-), pp. 243–60.

Dalton, P. and Nankivell, C. (2003) *HIMSS. Hybrid Information Management Skills for Senior Staff*, Birmingham: University of Central England Centre for Information Research.

Davidson, M.J. (2004) *Women in Management Worldwide*, Aldershot: Gower.

Davidson, M.J. and Cooper, C.L. (1992) *Shattering the Glass Ceiling: The Woman Manager*, London: Paul Chapman.

De'ath, E., et al. (2002) *Keynotes: Careers Information for Adults*, Trowbridge: Lifetime Careers Publishing.

de Board, R. (1987) *Counselling Skills*, Aldershot: Gower.

de Board, R. (1978) *The Psychoanalysis of Organizations*, London: Tavistock.

Department of Culture, Media and Sport (1999) *Libraries for all: social inclusion in public libraries: policy and guidance for local authorities in England*, London: DCMS.

Department of Culture, Media and Sport (2003) *Framework for the Future – Libraries, Learning and Information in the Next Decade*, London: DCMS.

Department for Education and Employment (1997) *Labour Market and Skills Trends, 1997–8*, Sheffield: DfEE.

Department for Education and Employment (1998) *The Learning Age: A Renaissance for a New Britain*, London: Stationery Office.

Department of Trade and Industry (1998) *Our Competitive Future: Building the Knowledge Economy*, London: Stationery Office. Cmnd. 4176.

Dikel, M.R. (2002) *Guide to Internet Job Searching*, Berkeley: Ten Speed Press.

Dixon, A. (2003) *Careers and Personal Advisers Handbook 2003–4*, London: Trotman.

Downey, M. (1999) *Effective Coaching*, London: Orion Business Books.

Drucker, P.F. (1995) *The Post Capitalist Society*, London: Butterworth-Heinemann.

Dupont-Joshua, A. (ed.) (2002) *Working Inter-culturally in Counselling Settings*, London: Brunner-Routledge.

Durcan, J. and Oates, D. (1996) *Career Paths for the 21st Century – How to Beat Job Insecurity*, London: Century.

Edwards, A. (2001) *Supporting Personal Advisers in Connexions: Perspectives on Supervision and Mentoring from Allied Professions*, Canterbury: Canterbury Christ Church University College.

Eichler, M. (1980) *The Double Standard*, London: Croom Helm.

Eraut, M. (1994) *Developing Professional Knowledge and Competence*, London: Falmer Press.

Exploring the learning community; report of the Education and Libraries Task Group to the Secretaries of State for Culture, Media and Sport and for Education and Employment, (2002) London: Library and Information Commission.

Fisher, B. (1994) *Mentoring*, London: Library Association.

Fisher, D.P. (1998) 'Is the librarian a distinct personality type?', *Journal of Librarianship and Information Science*, **20** (1) pp. 36–47.

Garrod, P. (1998) 'Skills for new information professions (SKIP): an evaluation of the key findings', *Program*, **32** (3) pp. 41–63.

Garrod, P. and Sidgreaves, I. (1997) *Skills for New Information Professionals: The Skip Project*, London: Library Information Technology Centre.

Gaskell, C. (2002) *Transform your Life*, London: Thorsons.

Gavin, B. (2003) 'Out of the chaos: progression and regression in the workplace', *Psychodynamic Practice*, **9** (1), February, pp. 43–60.

Gilchrist, A. and Mahon, B. (2003) *Information Architecture: Designing Information Environments for Purpose*, London: Facet Publishing.

'Giving progress a better chance' (2002) *Library and Information Appointments*, **5** (8), April, p. 1.

Gothard, B. (1999) 'Career as myth', *Psychodynamic Counselling*, **5** (1), pp. 87–97.

Goulding, A. et al. (1999) 'Supply and demand: the workforce needs of library and information services and personal qualities of new professionals', *Journal of Librarianship and Information Science*, **31**, pp. 212–23.

Goulding, A. and Kerslake, E. (1997) *Training for Part-Time and Temporary Workers*, London: Library Association Publishing.

'Graduates the market needs: how are universities keeping up with the changing market demand for skills', (2003) *Library and Information Update*, **2** (5), pp. 48–50.

Handy, C. (1990) *The Age of Unreason*, London: Arrow.

Handy, C. (1984) *The Future of Work: A Guide to a Changing Society*, Oxford, Blackwell.

Handy, C. (1993) *Understanding Organisations*, London: Penguin.

Hannabus, S. (1998) 'Flexible jobs: changing patterns in information and library work', *New Library World*, **99** (141), pp. 104–11.

Heery, W. (1994) 'Corporate mentoring can break the glass ceiling', *HR Focus*, May, pp. 17–18.

Hirschhorn, L. (1988) *The Workplace Within: Psychodynamics of Organizational Life*, London: MIT Press.

Hobsons' Guides to Careers in ... series (2003) London: Trotman.

Holden, J. (2002) *Cultural Leadership Initiative*, London: Clore Duffield Foundation.

Hood, V.G. (1995) 'Work-related counselling – a psychodynamic approach', *Psychodynamic Counselling*, **1** (2), pp. 239–52.

Hopkins, L. (2001) *What's Happening to the Careers Service in England?*, Stourbridge: Institute of Careers Guidance.

Hopson, B. and Scally, A. (1999) *Build your own Rainbow: a Workbook for Career and Life Management*, 3rd edn, Didcot, Management Books.

Horne, M. and Jones, D.S. (2001) *Leadership – The Challenge for All?*, Bedford: Institute of Management.

Houston, K. (1999) *Creating Winning CVs and Applications*, London: Trotman.

Howard, L. and Taw, R. (2001) *Key Skills Analysis: A Resource for Analysing Job Content and Training Needs and for Selecting, Training and Development Programmes*, Aldershot: Gower.

Huckle, M. (2002). 'Charter still central to CILIP', *Library Association Record*, **104** (2), p. 84.

Humphries, J. (1986) *Part-Time Work*, London: Kogan Page.

Hyams, E. (2002) 'Profile of Caroline Plumb', *Library and Information Update*, **1** (9), p. 26.

IFLA Membership Directory. http://www.ifla.org/database/directory.htm.

Industrial Society and the ITEM Group (1989) *The Line Manager's Role in Developing Talent: Coaching, Mentoring, Counselling*, London: Industrial Society.

'Information – a new value proposition – how information professionals can thrive in complex and constantly changing organisations' (2002) *Library and Information Update*, **1** (6), p. 8.

Information Services National Training Organisation (isNTO) (2000) *Information and Library Services National Occupational Standards*, London: isNTO.

Information Services National Training Organisation (isNTO) (2000) *Skills Foresight in the Information Services Sector, 2000–2007*, London: IsNTO.

Institute of Careers Guidance (1997) *A Career in Careers Guidance*, Stourbridge: Institute of Careers Guidance.

Institute of Careers Guidance (1997) *Occasional Papers in Careers Guidance. No. 2*, Stourbridge: Institute of Careers Guidance.

Institute of Careers Guidance (2002) *Careers Guidance: Constructing the Future – 2002*, Stourbridge: Institute of Careers Guidance.

Institute of Careers Guidance (2002) *Client Confidentiality: An ICG Briefing Paper*, Stourbridge: Institute of Careers Guidance.

Institute of Careers Guidance (2002) *One Aim, Three Routes: An ICG Briefing Paper*, Stourbridge: Institute of Careers Guidance.

Institute of Management/Demos (2001) *Leadership: the Challenge for All?*, London: Council for Excellence in Management and Leadership.

Institute of Race Relations (1998) *Race and Class: The Threat of Globalism*, London: Institute of Race Relations.

'It's happening now' (2002) *Library and Information Appointments*, **5** (23), pp. 1–2.

Jackson, T. and Jackson, E. (1991) *The Perfect CV*, London: Piatkus.

Javidan, M. (1998) 'Core competence: what does it mean in practice', *Long Range Planning*, **31** (1) pp. 60–71.

Johnstone, J. (1999) *Passing that interview*, London: How to Books.

Jones, R. (2004) *You Want to Work Where?*, London: Trotman.

Kakabadse, A., Bank, J. and Vinnicombe, S. (2004) *Working in Organisations*, Aldershot: Gower.

Kalseth, K., Cano, V. and Stanton, T. (1996) *New Roles and Challenges for Information Professionals in the Business Environment*, The Hague: International Federation for Information and Documentation (FID).

Kareem, J. and Littlewood, R., (eds) (2000) *Intercultural Therapy*, Oxford: Blackwell Science Ltd.

Kets de Vries, M.F.R. (1991) *Organisations on the Couch – Clinical Perspectives on Organisational Behaviour and Change*, Oxford: Jossey-Bass.

Khan, A. (2000). 'Stamping out institutional racism', *Library Association Record*, **102** (1) pp. 38–9.

Kidd, J.M. et al. (1994) 'Is guidance an applied science? The role of theory in the careers guidance interview', *British Journal of Guidance and Counselling*, **22** (3), pp. 385–403.

Kidd, J. (1996) *Rethinking Careers Education and Guidance*, London: Routledge.

Klein, M. (1975) *The Writings of Melanie Klein*, 4 volumes, London: Hogarth Press and Institute of Psychoanalysis.

Klein, M., Heimann, P. and Money-Kyrle, R. (eds) (1955) *New Directions in Psycho-analysis*, London: Basic Books.

Kolb, D. and Fry, R. (1975) 'Towards an applied theory of experiential learning', in Cooper, C.L. (ed.) *Theories of Group Process*, Chichester: Wiley.

Laing, R.D. (1960) *The Divided Self*, London: Tavistock.

Lank, E. (1997) 'Leveraging invisible assets: the human factor', *Long Range Planning Review*, **30** (3), pp. 406–12.

Laplanche, J. and Pontalis, J.B. (1988) *The Language of Psychoanalysis*, London: Karnac.

Leong, F.T.L. (ed.) (1995) *Career Development and Vocational Behaviour of Racial and Ethnic Minorities*, New Jersey: Lawrence Earlbaum Associates.

Levy, P. (1993) *Interpersonal Skills*, London: Library Association Publishing.

Lewis, N. (1999) 'Level 4 NVQs – an alternative route to professional status?', *Library Association Record*, **101** (2), pp. 94–6.

Library Association (1992) *The Framework for Continuing Professional Development: Your Personal Profile*, London: Library Association.

Library Association (2002) *Report of the Policy Advisory Group on a National Information Policy*, London: Library Association.

McDermott, E. (1998) 'A niceness of librarians: attitudinal barriers to career progression', *Library Management*, **19** (8), pp. 453–8.

McLeod, J. (1999) *Introduction to Counselling*, 2nd edn, Buckingham: Open University Press.

McLeod, J. and Machin, L. (1998) 'The context of counselling: a neglected dimension of training and practice', *British Journal of Guidance and Counselling*, **26** (3), pp. 325–36.

Maitland, I. (1997) *Your Mid-Career Shift*, London: Thorsons.

Manasseh, L. (2002) 'Connecting with career management', *Career Guidance Today*, **10** (1), pp. 26–7.

Marchand, D.A. (ed.) (2000) *Competing with Information*, Chichester: Wiley.

Marshall, J. (1984) *Women Managers: Travellers in a Male World*, Chichester, Wiley.

Matthews, S. (1997) *Mentoring and Coaching: The Essential Leadership Skills*, London: FT Pitman Publishing.

Miller, R. (1999) *Promoting Yourself at Interview*, London: Trotman.

Miller, J.S. and Cardy, R.L. (2000) 'Self monitoring and performance appraisal: rating outcomes in project teams', *Journal of Organizational Behaviour*, **21** (6), pp. 609–60.

Miller-Tiedman, A. (1999) *Learning, Practising and Living the New Careering*, London: Accelerated Development.

Minutes career kit (1997) London: Kogan Page.

Mitroff, I.I. (1989) *Stakeholders of the Organisational Mind*, London: Jossey-Bass.

Moore, N. (1999) 'Partners in the information society', *Library Association Record*, **101** (12), pp. 702–30.

Moore, B. and O'Neill, D. (1996) *Impact of Redundancies on Local Labour Markets and the Post-Redundancy Experience*, London: HMSO.

Mount, E. (ed.) (1997) *Expanding Technologies – Expanding Careers. Librarianship in Transition*, New York: Special Libraries Association.

Museums, Libraries and Archives Council (2004) *Investing in Knowledge*, London: MLA.

Muzzy, F. (2002) 'What employers really need', *Library and Information Appointments*, **5** (4), p. 1.

Nankivell, M.C. and Schoolbred, M. (1996) *Mentoring in Library and Information Services: An Approach to Staff Support*, London: British Library Research and Innovation Centre (Report RIC/G/296).

Neenan, M. (2001) *Life Coaching – A Cognitive Behavioural Approach*, London: Routledge Taylor and Francis.

Nickell, H. (2002) *Surfing Your Career*, 2nd edn, London: Trotman,

'No profession will undergo more radical change between 2000 and 2010 than will the Information Professional', (2001) *Information Outlook*, **4** (3) pp. 25–30.

Noonan, E. (1989) 'The personal significance of work', in Klein, L. (ed.) *Working with Organisations*, Luxwood, West Sussex: Kestrel Print.

Obholzer, A. and Roberts, V. (1994) *The Unconscious at Work: Individual and Organisation Stress in the Human Sciences*, London: Routledge and Kegan Paul.

Occupations 2003 (2002) London: Trotman.

Organization for Economic Cooperation and Development (OECD) (2000) *From Initial Education to Working Life: Making Transitions Work*, Paris: OECD.

Organization for Economic Cooperation and Development (OECD) (2001) *Knowledge and Skills for Life: First Results from PISA 2000*, Paris: OECD.

Open to All? The public library and social exclusion (2000) London: Re:source: Council for Museums, Archives and Libraries.

Osipow, S.H. and Fitzgerald, L.F. (1996) *Theories of Career Development*, 4th edn, Needham Heights: Allyn and Bacon.

Oxbrow, N. (2000) 'Skills and competencies to succeed in a knowledge economy', *Information Outlook,* **4** (10) pp. 18–20.

Pantry, S. (1997) 'Whither the information profession? Challenges and opportunities: the cultivation of information professionals for the new millennium', *Aslib Proceedings,* **49** (6), pp. 170–2.

Pantry, S. and Griffiths, P. (2003) *Your Essential Guide to Career Success*, London: Facet Publishing.

Peach, L. (1993) 'Planning careers', *Personnel Today*, 23 November, p. 15.

Pedlar, M. (ed.) (1983) *Action-Learning in Practice*, Aldershot: Gower.

Pedlar, M., Burgoyne, J. and Boydell, T. (1999) *The Learning Company*, London: McGraw Hill.

Poland, E., Curran, M. and Owens, R.G. (1995) *Women and Senior Management: A Research Study of Career Barriers and Progression in the Library and Information Sector, Final Report*, London: Library Association.

Polkinghorne, D.E. (1988) *Narrative Knowing and the Human Sciences*, Albany: State University of New York.

Prospects: A Strategy for Action: Library and Information Research, Development and Innovation in the United Kingdom, (1998) London: Library and Information Commission Research Committee.

Quenk, N.L. (1996) *In the Grip: Our Hidden Personality*, Palo Alto: Consulting Psychologists Press Inc.

Rajan, A. (1992) *Where will the New Jobs be?*, Stourbridge: Institute of Careers Guidance.

Rajan, A. (1996) *Leading People*, Tunbridge Wells: Create.

Rajan, A., Van Eupen, P. and Jaspers, A. (1998) *Britain's Flexible Labour Market: What Next?*, Stourbridge: Institute of Careers Guidance.

Regan, J. (2003) 'Mentoring schemes: raising the standards', *Library and Information Update,* **2** (4), pp. 36–7.

Revans, R.W. (1980) *Action Learning: New Techniques for Management*, London: Blond and Briggs.

Rice, A.K. (1965) *Learning for Leadership*, London: Tavistock.

Rogers, C. (1961) *On Becoming a Person*, Boston: Houghton Mifflin.

Sampson, E. (2002) *Build your Personal Brand*, 3rd edn, London: Kogan Page.

Savickas, M.L. (1993) 'Career counselling in the postmodern era', *Journal of Cognitive Psychotherapy,* **7** (3), pp. 205–15.

Schein, E.H (1985) *Organisational Culture and Leadership*, New York: Jossey-Bass.

Schein, E.H. (1990) *Career Anchors*, New York: Jossey-Bass.

Sconul. *Information support for eLearning principles and practice* (2003) [http://www.sconul.ac.uk/news/ukeu]

Second Chances: national guide to education and training for adults, (2002) Trowbridge: Lifetime Careers Publishing.

Segal, H. (1973) *Introduction to the Work of Melanie Klein*, London: Hogarth Press.

Seligman, L. (1994) *Developmental Career Counselling and Assessment*, London: Sage.

Senge, P.M. (1994) *The Fifth Discipline: The Art and Practice of the Learning Organisation*, New York: Doubleday.

Sharpe, D. et al. (2003) 'Cross-sectoral staff development', *Library and Information Update*, **2** (8), p. 5.

Sharing skills: an evaluation (2002) London: Re:source: Council for Museums, Archives and Libraries.

Sharon, J. et al. (2000) 'Identifying the key people in your KM effort: the role of human knowledge intermediaries', *Knowledge Management Review*, **3** (3), November/December, pp. 26–9.

Shaw, L. (1996) *Telecommute! Go to Work Without Leaving Home*, Chichester: Wiley.

Shaw, M. (ed.) (1981) *Recent Advances in Personal Construct Technology*, Cambridge Academic Press.

Smith, C. and Crommentuijn, P. (2001) *Crazy Paving – The Indispensable Guide to Developing your Career*, Bedford: Institute of Management.

Snyder, R.A. (1993) 'The glass ceiling for women: things that don't cause it and things that won't break it', *Human Resource Development Quarterly*, **4** (1), pp. 97–103.

Soft skills; hard facts: a nationwide investigation into a key skill area (1997) London: Austin Knight in collaboration with People Management.

Sohn, L. (1985) 'Narcissistic organization, projective identification, and the formation of the identificate', *International Journal of Psycho-Analysis*, **66** (-), pp. 201–13.

Sonnenberg, D. (1997) 'The "new career" changes: understanding and managing anxiety', *British Journal of Guidance and Counselling*, **25** (4), pp. 463–72.

Special Libraries Association (1991) *Future Competencies of the Information Profession*, Washington DC: Special Libraries Association.

Spiegel, H. and Spiegel, D. (1978) *Trance and Treatment*, New York: Basic Books.

Stapley, C. (1996) *The Personality of the Organisation*, London: Free Association Books.

Stenson, A., Raddon, R. and Abell, A. (1999) *Skills and Competencies in the Corporate Sector*, London: British Library Research and Innovation Centre.

Stewart, T. (2001) *The Wealth of Knowledge*, London: Nicholas Brealey.

Storr, A. (1963) *The Integrity of the Personality*, Harmondsworth: Penguin.

Storr, A. (1989) *Solitude*, London: Harper Collins, Flamingo.

Strategy for research for DCMS 2003–2005/6. Technical paper no. 3 (2003) London: DCMS.

Sultana, R.G. (2003) *Guidance Policies in the Knowledge Society: Trends, Challenges and Responses across Europe*, Thessaloniki: European Centre for the Development of Vocational Training.

Super, D.E. (1957) *Psychology of Careers*, New York: Harper and Row.

Sutton, B. (2000) *Career Networking: Networking for Career and Job Success*, London: Industrial Society.

Symington, N. (1986) *The Analytic Experience*, London: Free Association Books.

Taylor, G. (2003) 'At the career crossroads', *Library and Information Appointments*, **6** (19), pp. 1–2.

TFPL (1999) *Skills for Knowledge Management: Building a Knowledge Economy*, London: TFPL.

TFPL (annual) *TFPL CKO Summit: Knowledge Management in the Public Sector*, London: TFPL.

TFPL (2003) *Knowledge and Information Management Competency Dictionary*, London: TFPL.

TFPL (2003) *Knowledge and Information Skills Toolkit*, London: www.tfpl.com.

Thebridge, S. and Hartland-Fox, R. (2003) 'Evaluating in the electronic world', *Library and Information Update*, **2** (3), pp. 48–9.

Tjosvold, D. and Leung, K. (eds) (2003) *Cross-cultural Management*, Aldershot: Gower.

Training and Development Directory 2004, www.cilip.org.uk/training.

Trask, M. and Wood, J. (1984) *Career Planning and Assessment for Librarians*, Lindfield, NSW: College of Advanced Education.

Trickey, K.V.C. (2003) 'One day can make a real difference: renegotiating the working week', *Personnel, Training and Education*, **19** (3), pp. 1–2.

Trompenaars, A. et al. (1997) *Riding the Waves of Culture: Understanding Cultural Diversity in Global Business*, 2nd edn, London: Nicholas Brealey.

Usherwood, B. (1998) 'Recruiting a first class workforce', *Library Association Record Supplement*, **1** (19), p. 1.

Usherwood, Bob et al. (2001) *Recruit, Retain, Lead: The Public Library Workforce Study*, Library and Information Commission Research Report 106. London: Re:source: The Council for Museums, Archives and Libraries.

Wall, J.T. and Loewenthal, D. (1998) 'Unlimited power – encountering narcissism in career development counselling', *Psychodynamic Counselling*, **4** (1), February, pp. 33–54.

Ward, S. (1998) 'Educators, gatekeepers, advisers, explorers, organisers and engineers, analysts and assessors', *Inform*, **209** (11), p. 12.

Watts, A.G. (1983) *Education, Unemployment and the Future of Work*, Milton Keynes: Open University Press.

Watts, A.G. (1999) *Reshaping Career Development for the 21st Century*, Derby: Centre for Guidance Studies.

Watts, A.G. et al. (1996) *Rethinking Careers Education and Guidance: Theory, Policy and Practice*, London: Routledge.

Whapham, J. and Brindle, L.R. (2004) 'What do you enjoy? A career counselling inventory', *Selection and Development Review*, **20** (2), pp. 18–23.

Whiddett, S. and Hollyforde, S. (1999) *The Competencies Handbook*, London: Chartered Institute of Personnel and Development.

Williams, P. and Quinsee, S. (2003) 'Using Web CT to teach key skills', *Library and Information Update*, **2** (2), pp. 42–3.

Williamson, M. (1993) *Training Needs Analysis*, London: Library Association Publishing.

Willis, I. and Daisley, J. (1990) *Springboard: Women's Development Workbook*, Stroud: Hawthorn Press.

Winnicott, D.W. (1964) *The Child, the Family and the Outside World*, London: Penguin.

Winnicott, D.W. (1965) *The Maturational Processes and the Facilitating Environment*, London: Hogarth Press and Institute of Psycho-Analysis.

Winnicott, D.W. (1988) *Human Nature*, London: Free Association Books.

Wintermann, V. et al. (2003) 'A new kind of worker', *Library and Information Update*, **2** (10) pp. 38–9.

Wood, R. and Payne, T. (1998) *Competency Based Recruitment and Selection: A Practical Guide*, Chichester: Wiley.

Yate, M. and Dourlain, T. (2002) *Online Job Hunting*, London: Trotman.

Journals

Aslib Proceedings	http://www.aslib.co.uk/proceedings/
British Journal of Guidance and Counselling	http://ndf.co.uk/journals/titles/
	http://www.tandf.co.uk/journals/titles/
Business Archives Council	http://www.archives.gla.ac.uk/bac/
Business Information Review	http://www.bowker.com/bowkerweb/catalog2001/prod00067.htm/
Career Guidance Today	http://www.icg-uk.org/
Computer Business Review	http://www.cbronline.com/index.htm/
The Daily Telegraph	http://jobs.telegraph.co.uk/
E Content	http://www.econtentmag.com/
E-Learning Age	http://www.elearningage.co.uk/
The Economist	http://www.economist.com/
The Guardian	http://www.jobs.guardian.co.uk/
Harvard Business Review	http://harvardbusinessonline.hbsp.harvard.edu/b01/en/hbr/hbr_home.jhtml
Health Service Journal	http://www.hsj.co.uk/
HR Focus	http://www.emeraldinsight.com/
HR Professional	http://www.hrprof.com/
Human Resource Development Quarterly	http://www.wileyeurope.com/cda/sec/0,616200.html/
Human Resource Management Review	http://www.hrmanagementreview.com/
Human Resource Professional (now HR Professional)	http://www.humanresourcesmagazines.com/
Inform	http://www.ijs.org.uk/
Information Career Trends	http://www.Lisjobs.com/
Information Outlook	http://www.sla.org/content/Shop/Information/ioarticles/index.cfm/

Information Strategy	http://www.auerbach-publications.com/
Information Today	http://www.infotoday.com/IT/default.shtml/
Information World Review	http://www.iwr.co.uk/
Intellectual Asset Management	http://www.globewhitepage.com/iam/?r=222
International Journal of Psychoanalysis	http://www.ijpa.org/
Internet World	http://www.internetworld.com/
Journal of Clinical Psychology	http://www.bps.org.uk/
Journal of Librarianship and Information Science	http://www.bowker.com/bowkerweb.catalogue.200/
Journal of Organisational Behaviour	http://www.interscience.wiley.com/
Knowledge Management Review	http://www.km-review.com/
Library and Information Appointments (now Library and Information Update)	http://www.cilip.org.uk/update/
Library and Information Gazette	debbyraven@btconnect.com
Library Management	http://www.emeraldinsight.com/
Long Range Planning	http://www.lrp.ac/
Long Range Planning Review	http://www.lrp.ac/Review/
Managing Information	http://www.managinginformation.com/
New Library World	http://www.emeraldinsight.com/
New Scientist	http://www.newscientistjobs.com/
Personnel Today	http://www.personneltoday.com/
Personnel Training and Education Group (PTEG)	http://www.cilip.org.uk/groups/pteg/
Program	http://www.emeraldinsight.com
Psychodynamic Counselling	http://www.tandf.co.uk/
Psychodynamic Practice	http://www.tandf.co.uk/
Public Administration and Public Policy	http://www.dekker.com/
Records Management Bulletin	http://www.rms-gb.org.uk/
Recruitment Consultant	http://www.recruitmentconsultant.co.uk/
Re:source News	http://www.resource.gov.uk/news/index.asp/
Selection and Development Review	http://www.bps.org.uk/
State Librarian	http://www.circleofstatelibrarians.co.uk/
The Times	http://www.timesonline.co.uk/
Times Higher Education Supplement	http://www.thesjobs.co.uk/

Index